GW00691326

# contents

# 2 ONE PEOPLE:
## IN THE PENTATEUCH

ONE

One Holy, Catholic, Apostolic People

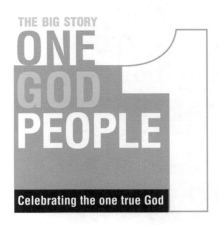

# Spring Harvest 2007

# STUDY GUIDE

## by Jeff Lucas

The author would like to express his thanks to the following, who have all made valuable contributions to the Spring Harvest 2007 Study Guide.

Luke Bretherton, Stephen Gaukroger, Ernest Lucas, Nims Obunge, Jonathan Oloyede, Ian Stackhouse and members of the Spring Harvest Leadership Team: Pete Broadbent, Steve Chalke, Ian Coffey, Ruth Dearnley, Alan Johnson, Rachael Orrell, Russell Rook.

"I am God. I have called you to live right and well. I have taken responsibility for you, kept you safe. I have set you among my people to bind them to me, **and provided you as a lighthouse to the nations**, to make a start at bringing people into the open, into light: opening blind eyes, releasing prisoners from dungeons, emptying the dark prisons. I am God."

*– Isaiah 42:5–8, The Message*

But **you are a chosen people**, a royal priesthood, a holy nation, a people belonging to God, that you may declare the praises of him who called you out of darkness into **his wonderful light. Once you were not a people, but now you are the people of God**; once you had not received mercy, but now you have received mercy. Dear friends, I urge you, as aliens and strangers in the world, to abstain from sinful desires, which war against your soul. Live such good lives among the pagans that, though they accuse you of doing wrong, they may see your good deeds and glorify God on the day he visits us.

*– 1 Peter 2:9–12*

# 2 ONE PEOPLE: IN THE PENTATEUCH

**Today's goal** – explore the effect of the loss of God's Big Story and to see the potential for the church as we rediscover it.

## Teaching Block 1:

**People carriers:** truth incarnated through community

Teaching Block 1: Our aim is to regain the corporate and community perspective on God's relationships with humanity throughout history, without losing sight of the individual.

## Teaching Block 2:

**Israel, people for all peoples:** election's purpose, continuity and optimism

Teaching Block 2: Our aim is to explore the election of Israel and as a result to understand that God called and chose Israel, not at the expense of the rest, but for the sake of the rest.

## Teaching Block 3:

**One people, called to participate in and rehearse God's story:** the power of remembering

Teaching Block 3: "'The Word became flesh,' St. John said. And the church has turned flesh back into words." – Tom Wright. Our aim is to realise the impact of this quote and how we can remember who we really are. To begin to see how all the different aspects of our story can be creatively lived out by the church remembering, passing the story on, being committed to renewal, and engaging with people of all ages.

**One** Holy, Catholic, Apostolic People

# One people – the people of God in the Pentateuch

## Introduction

### Prelude: a righteous riot

On reaching Jerusalem, Jesus entered the temple area and began driving out those who were buying and selling there. He overturned the tables of the money changers and the benches of those selling doves, and would not allow anyone to carry merchandise through the temple courts. And as he taught them, he said, "Is it not written: 'My house will be called a house of prayer for all nations'? But you have made it 'a den of robbers.'"

*– Mark 11:15–17*

To onlookers, it must have seemed that a madman was on the loose.

The temple area in Jerusalem has been called 'thirty acres of piety and power'[1]. In Jesus' day it was the epicentre of Jewish national life. The temple boasted towering walls that soared to heights of three hundred feet; some of the larger stones in the walls weighed more than thirty tons. The Jews had a proverb: 'He who has not seen the holy place in its detailed construction has never seen a splendid building in his life.'[2] The temple was the pride and joy of many, an enduring symbol of national hope in a time of Roman occupation and oppression[3] with a staff of 18,000 priests and Levites.

During the annual festivals of pilgrimage, Jerusalem's population of 25,000 swelled to a teeming mass of 180,000 people[4]. The temple was home to the Sanhedrin, a 70-member council that was the final Jewish authority in all matters religious, civil and political. The Roman military kept an eagle eye on the temple area, fearing that trouble might ignite there: 500–600 soldiers were housed nearby.

**It was here, in the temple courts, that Jesus planned his holy assault.** Having carefully surveyed the terrain the night before (Mark 11:11), he burst into the outer area. Coins were strewn all over the stone floors, tables tumbled noisily and birds fluttered away in a flurry of feathers. For a while, all temple operations were suspended.

What was it that made Jesus so angry? At first glance, it seems that the money changers had provoked his ire. With their spiralling exchange rates and rip-off practices, the changers were fleecing sincere worshippers – it warranted a whipping. But there's more.

Most commentators believe that the traders had set up their stalls in the Court of the Gentiles[5]. The only place where non-Jews could gather had been turned into a noisy, overcrowded thoroughfare. In Mark's Gospel, Jesus declares that the temple was always intended as a 'house of prayer for all nations' (Isa 56:7, Mark 11:17). The priests had turned into robbers who stole the possibility of God from the Gentiles. Israel was called to be a prophetic signpost to the world, but instead she acted as if she owned the franchise on God and had 'shut the kingdom of heaven in [the] faces' of those who needed him most (Matt 23:13).

As we will see later in more detail, God's *election* (choice or selection) of Israel was his decision that this tiny people be a *channel* of salvation to all the earth, not just a model of what salvation looked like. And ultimately the message would be punched home through Israel's *eschatology* (their unfolding future, and indeed the future of the whole world, especially relating to the future spoken of by the prophets and fulfilled in Messianic hope). It was hoped that the history of Israel would march towards an epic climax, when they would be miraculously saved by God's intervention. That salvation work would lead the wider world to the true God. And of course, the great saving work of the Cross did take place in Israel – but that was a redeeming event Israel had not anticipated.

"The creator God has purposed from the beginning to address and deal with the problems within his creation through Israel… . Yahweh had chosen Israel for the sake of the wider world. Election, the choice of Israel, was the focal point of the divine purpose to act within the world to rescue and heal the world, to bring about what some biblical writers speak of as a 'new creation.'"
— *N.T. Wright*[6]

"A people who were meant to be a 'light to the Gentiles', bringing salvation to the ends of the earth (Isa 49:6), had become centred on their own separateness from those same Gentiles; those who were the guardians of the temple were only concerned with maintaining their own purity, their own ethnic boundaries, and keeping strangers out rather than welcoming them in."
— *Graham Tomlin*[7]

"The temple had become a symbol of resistance to the Gentiles rather than their inclusion in God's kingdom."
— *Marcus Borg*[8]

And so Jesus astonishingly called time on the temple, not just because of monetary corruption but also because it had come to represent the tragedy that God's 'people of God' project had stalled, because God's people had so misunderstood his intentions. Israel had lost the plot. And so Jesus took radical action.

"When we stay focused on the Jesus we meet in the New Testament, we discover no 'gentle Jesus, meek and mild', but one who grabs us by the scruff of the neck to shake loose from us all false images of deity we have cherished, one who is the great iconoclast smashing to bits our trivial gods."
— *Donald McCullough*[9]

The day before cleansing the temple, Jesus cursed a symbol of the temple, a fig tree (Mark 11:12–14). The next day, after the spectacular events of the courtyard, Jesus and his disciples passed by the tree and found it withered (Mark 11:20). The mighty building still stood, but it was doomed. Within a few years, it would be reduced to rubble. **Within a few days, Jesus would make a way for all people from every tribe, tongue and nation to become a part of the one people of God – and so the thick veil in the temple's holy of holies would be ripped apart by an unseen hand (Mark 15:38).**

So it is that Peter celebrates the wonderful privilege that is ours today in and through Christ:

"But you are a chosen people, a royal priesthood, a holy nation, a people belonging to God, that you may declare the praises of him who called you out of darkness into his wonderful light. Once you were not a people, but now you are the people of God."
— *1 Peter 2:9*

**The big question remains: as part of the church universal, and the church triumphant, we are the people of God as those who are among the living children of Abraham. Will we live the story or are we in danger of losing the plot, too?**

## Our objective this week: not just gathering information, but sparking imagination

The third film in the *Lord of the Rings* trilogy created quite a stir among J.R.R. Tolkien purists. According to critics, a vital seven minutes of the final cut of the film was edited out. This not only changed the entire story, but altered the message of the film. The loss of a story changes everything.

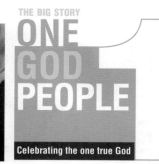
**At Spring Harvest 2006, we began our three-year journey to look at The Big Story: One God, One People, One Hope. This week, we have gathered to remind ourselves that we are the people of what Tom Wright calls 'the big fat story'. That huge story defines who we are, and why we live as we do. It is the reason for our values, our hopes and dreams. It is the reason for the church.** Jacques Ellul, one of the most perceptive Christian commentators on church and society in the twentieth century, called on the church to refuse to give in to the 'tired old stories of the world around them'.[10] **Far from being a tale of mere existence and survival, the big fat story of the people of God is a widescreen big-picture epic, a captivating blockbuster.**

"If you are a Christian, the story that tells you who you are is not the story of your parents, ancestors, ethnic group or social class. It is, instead, the story of the Bible – the promise to Abraham, deliverance from slavery to Egypt and sin, and the gift of land to landless Israelites and life to dead sinners. This story of promise, deliverance and gift is your family history, the story that defines you."
– *Graham Tomlin*[11]

"It is of the very essence of the Christian journey that we are a storied people. Like our Jewish forefathers, we are shaped by the stories of God's actions in history. And just as the Hebrew slaves were given the enactment of the Passover and told to 'tell this to your children', so we are called to re-enact and re-tell the story of Jesus over and over. The great dramatic events of scripture tell the story of a God who time and again chooses grace over karma; who breaks into history to make losers winners; who chooses the ultimate act of self-emptying as the central drama of his own life."
– *Gerard Kelly*[12]

**We must allow that story to grip us again.** Bishop Graham Cray describes a student who after hearing a presentation of the gospel said: "It doesn't seem real. It seems true, but it doesn't seem real."[13] The story must be not only true but also real to us if it is to seem anything more than antiquated fiction when we share it with our world.

But if that is to happen we must do more than gather information, even correct theological information. We must allow God's Spirit to stir our imaginations again. **Faith requires imagination, an ability to dream, the fuel for passion and commitment.** Without that stirring, we will settle into the mundane drudgery of tedious functionality. We will be faithful but weary souls, doing what we do (and perhaps what we have always done) but forgetting why we do what we do.

In Bruce Chatwin's *The Songlines* an Irish priest describes the connection between faith and imagination: "Flynn has to be some kind of genius… but I don't think he was ever a believer. He could never take the leap into faith. Didn't have the imagination for it."[14]

"Listening to or reading a story is not primarily an application of intellect. It is an act of shared imagination. In story, one is invited (not coerced) into a different world through the act of active imagining."
– *Michael Riddell*[15]

**For some of us, the 'old, old story' of the gospel has got old: we are bored believers; we have lost the gift of astonishment, and grace isn't so amazing any more.** God helping us we must connect with the Big Story afresh, for it is, as C.S. Lewis said, 'the great story'. When Lewis came to the conclusion of his *Chronicles of Narnia*, he noted: 'This is the end of all the stories.' But for the Narnia characters, he described an ongoing, breathtaking destiny.

"It was only the beginning of the real story…. Now at last they were beginning chapter one of the Great Story, which no one on earth has read: which goes on forever: in which every chapter is better than the one before."[16]

Our time together is an opportunity for us to allow our imaginations to be stirred once more.

And this is the story that remains unfinished, but most unusually, not in its ending but in its current unfolding. We know the beginning (the Creation), the middle (the Cross) and the end of the story (the creation of a New Heaven and a New Earth). **But our part in the plot is still being written, and what will be penned is contingent upon our response to the plot and the Great Director himself.** Tom Wright describes the story of God's purposes as being a five-act drama in which we are invited to improvise our part in Act Five.[17]

"In God's story… the piece between Jesus and his work on the cross and the final chapter is still being written. God's story is not just about what God has done, but also about what God… is doing now. God is still writing the story, and, incredibly, God has invited us to participate in that writing." – *Bryant L. Myers*[18]

## The specifics: considering one holy catholic apostolic church

In AD 381, the church was under threat from schism and false teaching. What is now popularly known as *The Nicene Creed* was developed as representative bishops met in Constantinople (although there is no evidence that the creed reached its current form until AD 451). *The Nicene Creed* calls us to affirm that 'we believe in one holy catholic and apostolic church'. That summary phrase will provide the framework for our time together.

**Today, we'll consider the people of God in the Pentateuch (the first five books of the Bible).** We'll see that we are *one*, an elected (chosen) people. Election was a *corporate* act, and we'll see that God always fulfils his purposes through communities. The election of Israel was also a *hopeful* act – obviously the idea of a people being appointed to bring radical change on the earth implies a belief that the world can be changed by the presence of a chosen people. We'll ask: Do we still believe that we can affect our world? We'll also consider that there is potential for change only as long as we are people of the self-revelation of God, and that this is the foundation for God's people everywhere at all times. **This is the big story that we must continually rehearse**

to each other, and proclaim and act out to our confused world, which is so awash with bogus tales. As we remember all that God has done, we are renewed to imagine and serve again.

We are called to be one **holy** people, distinctly different and commanded to walk in the ways of our holy God. In our religious acts, and in the ethical lifestyle practices that should accompany and follow our worship (as part of it), we are to be a people apart – not separatists but a 'shalom' people, the dynamic working model for how life on earth was designed to be lived. **We shall carefully consider the challenge and invitation to holiness on Day Three, as we look at the people of God in the histories and prophets.**

We are called to be a **catholic** or universal people, never existing for the sake of ourselves but created for all creation to see the rule and reign (or kingdom) of God established in all places at all times. Thus the people of God are always concerned about those on the margins. **We shall look closer at what it means to emulate the inclusive embrace that was the ministry and message of Jesus as we continue our journey on Day Four.**

We are called to be an **apostolic church** – a sent travelling community organized around a mission and committed to the developmental maturity of the people of God as disciples. **We shall look at the apostolic church of Paul and other New Testament writers on Day Five.**

We're looking at the **church** over all four days because, as we'll see, the people of God throughout the ages were always called the 'church' (though they started in the synagogue!) – the *ekklesia*, a gathering of people who are called to God and for God.

**Each session has opportunities for individual personal reflections (person to person) as well as group discussions (small groups). There will be pauses for prayer.**

## Pause for Prayer: Cooperating with the grace conspiracy

Right at the start of our journey we are confronted by a Jesus who is willing to challenge the greatest power structures and uproot and overthrow some of the most cherished aspects of heritage and tradition. Nothing, not even the revered temple, was off limits to him. Let's pause and offer God an 'access all areas' pass to our lives, practices, convictions and prejudices. As we pause to pray, let's remind ourselves of the potential of this moment, and of these days we spend together. As David Hubbard has put it, "In a massive conspiracy of grace, Father, Son and Spirit have plotted together to turn our lives around."[19]

### Mighty God,

We come before you, and offer ourselves to you.

Step freely, Lord, into the courts of our lives, not as a surprising invader, but as our welcomed Lord.

Bring your loving disruption, your all-wise revelation, and where necessary, your acts of holy demolition.

Scatter the chattels of mere religion that only serve to blind our world to your light and bar so many to your loving kindness.

Turn the tables on us, and be Lord where we have set up our stalls of rebellion and selfishness.

Kindle the fire of your love in our hearts again; grant us the gift to imagine. Dream your dreams through us.

Show us your ways, and be Lord of our journeying.

In the name of Christ,

*Amen.*

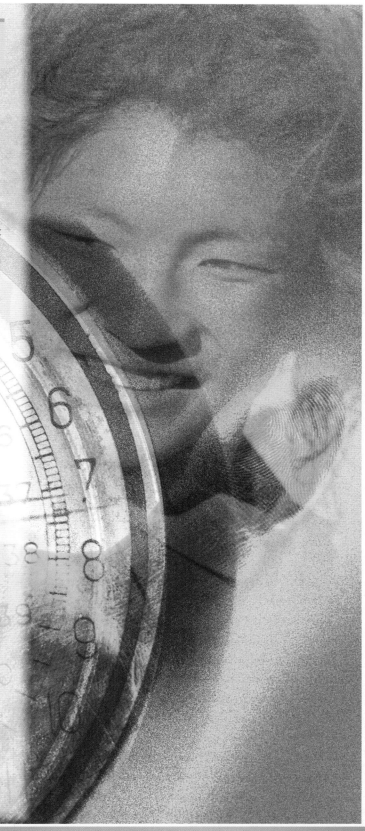

# People Carriers: Truth Incarnated Through Community

## Sin quake at Babel: prevailing chaos

"There is no lighthouse keeper. There is no lighthouse. There is no dry land. There are only people living on rafts made from their own imaginations. And there is the sea."
– *John Dominic Crossan*[20]

The eleventh chapter of Genesis – the Tower of Babel account – describes a climax of sin as rebellious humankind teeters on the brink of forming a dark collaboration, a collective clenched fist waved in the face of God. The effects of sin had reached global proportions. The Tower of Babel symbolized the human compulsion to 'make a name for ourselves' (Gen 11:4) and construct something from the ground up that 'reaches to the heavens'. It symbolized worship that places humanity, and not God, at its foundation and centre. This was a revolt against God, a storming of the gates of heaven by humans wanting to be God.

Against this backdrop of chaos and judgement our ever-patient God chose to activate the next phase of his 'One People' plan; this was the moment for elderly Abraham and unexpectedly pregnant Sarah to discover their remarkable destiny to be the parents of a people who would become the carriers and conduits of the Big Story.

In the same way today, when chaos and confusion abounds, the 'one people of God' are desperately needed.

"A sense of a lack of depth, a lack of reality pervades this culture so much that no one quite knows any more what is real and what is fake… this nostalgia for reality is one of the key hallmarks of the postmodern world."
– *Graham Tomlin*[21]

"None of our societies know how to manage their mourning for the real."
– *Jean Baudrillard*[22]

*Bridget Jones's Diary*,[23] "**Monday 3 March: Weight: 9 stone 5 (hideous instant fat production after lard-smeared parental Sunday lunch), cigarettes 17 (emergency), incidents during parental lunch suggesting there is any sanity or reality remaining in life: 0.**"

## Rolling Stones and the search for meaning

The relentless search for meaning is as old as the hills. Greek mythology tells the story of the hapless Sisyphus, who incurred the wrath of the gods when he whispered secrets to humans that were supposed to be privy only to celestial beings. Punishment for Sisyphus was being sentenced to numbing meaninglessness. He had to roll a massive stone to the top of a hill, watch it roll down again, and then repeat the exercise – for ever.

Our culture of meaninglessness and uncertainty urgently needs the one people of God worldwide to live and speak with clarity and compassion. We live in turbulent days. While Christians are quite wrong to suggest that our

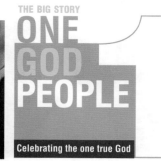

culture has no values (Make Poverty History and Live 8 are but two examples that prove this charge to be false), postmodernism has effectively removed the possibility of a foundational story being at the core of life.

We have data overload, but no story. We are awash with information, much of which is useless for solving even basic problems – and we are starved of substantial meaning and direction. Veteran American newscaster Ted Koppel addressed his colleagues in an acceptance speech when presented with the 'Broadcaster of the Year' award in 1986.

**"We have now become so obsessed with facts that we have lost all touch with truth. … Almost everything that is publicly said these days is recorded. Almost nothing of what is said is worth remembering."[24]**

Meaninglessness seeps into our domestic lives. Jose Martinez, a taxi driver in New York, provides a sound bite of despair:

**"We're here to die, just live and die. I live driving a cab. I do some fishing, take my girl out, pay taxes, do a little reading, and then get ready to drop dead. Life is a big fake. You're rich or you're poor. You're here, you're gone. You're like the wind. After you've gone, other people will come. It's too late to make it better. Everyone's fed up, can't believe in nothing no more. People have no pride. People have no fear! People only care about one thing and that's money. We're gonna destroy ourselves, nothing we can do about it. The only cure for the world's illness is nuclear war – wipe everything out and start over. We've become like a cornered animal, fighting for survival. Life is nothing."[25]**

Into this vacuum hurry storytellers eager to take the stage, some of them hawking tales of hopelessness. Philosophers speak of the 'silence of God' (Sartre) and the 'absence of God' (Jaspers); theologians have spoken of the 'eclipse of God' (Buber) and even the 'death of God' (Hamilton).[26]

Some scientists have joined the nihilistic chorus, such as Professor Richard Dawkins (as we noted during Spring Harvest 2006) and the late Stephen Jay Gould (a palaeontologist who summarized the 'reasons' for human life).

**"We are here because one odd group of fishes had a peculiar fin anatomy that could transform into legs for terrestrial creatures; because the earth never froze entirely during an ice age; because a small and tenuous species, arising in Africa a quarter of a million years ago, has managed, so far, to survive by hook and by crook. We may yearn for a 'higher' answer – but none exists."**
– *Stephen Jay Gould*[27]

**We must not give in to the temptation to always give science a bad press by exclusively focusing on those prominent scientists who take a nihilistic view.** Their view does not arise from science itself but from materialistic humanism, which Dawkins, for example, brings

> **God's answer to the international blight of sin was a new community, a new nation.**

to his understanding of the world in general, including his science. There are other scientists, who, though not Christians, see evidence of meaning and purpose in the picture that science paints of the universe.

Perhaps we should not be intimidated when certain scientists try to tell us the story. Michael Polanyi was a professor of Physical Chemistry and of Social Sciences at the University of Manchester, a fellow of Merton College, Oxford, and a fellow of The Royal Society. He warned his colleagues of the danger of their destroying the meaning of life by reducing everything to mere matter. As Ravi

# 2 ONE PEOPLE: IN THE PENTATEUCH

Zacharias says, "When science overplays its hand, it picks its own pockets."[28] But the result of that cultural pick-pocketing is the erosion of hope.

**Hopelessness is a fertile breeding ground for extremism.** If matter is everything and nothing really matters, then we are just pragmatic predators bent only on survival at whatever cost. Richard Dawkins admits, terrifyingly, that his conviction that humanity is nothing more than a machine created by genes means that ethics are illogical.

"Universal love and welfare of the species as a whole are concepts which simply do not make evolutionary sense." – *Dawkins*[29]

Confusingly, Dawkins does include some ethics in some of his work, for example in *The God Delusion*.[30]

This kind of despair, which is reflected in the music of Shostakovich and upon the bleak canvases of Mark Rothko and Edvard Munch, provides a thunderdome where extremism of all kinds can arise and call human life cheap and dispensable. Friedrich Nietzsche's 'death of God' and 'superman' philosophies and Karl Marx's politics that dismiss religion as 'the illusory sun which revolves around man as long as he does not revolve around himself' helped to usher in a global disaster.

"Nietzsche and Marx actually opened the floodgates to barbarity and violence on a scale unprecedented in history. … At the very point at which people aspired to become like God, Europe fell under the control of fascism, Nazism and Stalinism." – *David Smith*[31]

In the wake of the London bombings of 2005, we are sobered by a recent survey that suggests one in six British Muslims views the bombers as martyrs. The increasing popularity of the British National Party, with its thinly veiled fascist message, gives great cause for concern. In a culture stranded in the fog banks of confusion, urgent and desperate voices find a readier hearing. The people of the story are greatly needed.

## How God connects: individual and community

**Babel** signalled the curse of **judgement**:

"So the Lord scattered them from there over all the earth, and they stopped building the city. That is why it was called Babel—because there the Lord confused the language of the whole world. From there the Lord scattered them over the face of the whole earth." – *Genesis 11:8–9*

Abraham's call, and the ultimate creation of Israel, signalled God's intention to bring about blessing throughout the earth:

"The Lord had said to Abram, 'Leave your country, your people and your father's household and go to the land I will show you. I will make you into a great nation and I will bless you; I will make your name great, and you will be a blessing. I will bless those who bless you, and whoever curses you I will curse; and all peoples on earth will be blessed through you.'" – *Genesis 12:1–3*

As the story unfolds through Abraham, Isaac, Jacob, the formation of twelve tribes, the harsh persecution in Egypt, and then the epic Exodus and the gathering together at Mount Sinai, we see not just the rescue of a huge number of refugees, but the birth of a community created for the purposes of God in the earth. Although God deals with individuals, he calls us as individuals to connect with our destiny in and through community. We worship the proactive God, who reaches out to head us off on the pathway that we all walk in sin and towards judgement.

"God's answer to the international blight of sin was a new community, a nation that would be the pattern and model of redemption, as well as the vehicle by which the blessing of redemption would eventually embrace the rest of (hu)mankind." – *Chris Wright*[32]

"The Old Testament knows nothing, in any situation or at any time, of a religious individualism which gives

**One** Holy, Catholic, Apostolic People

a human a private relationship with God either in its roots, its realization or its goal. Just as it is in the formation of a divine society which gives meaning to the divine demand that summons the individual and enlists him or her in its service, so it is in serving his brethren that the obedience of the one who is called is proved, it is in the common cultic festivals that his religious life finds its natural expression, and it is towards a perfected people of God that his hope is directed."
– *Walther Eichrodt*[33]

"Pick up a hymn book … . Note how very many 'I' and 'my' hymns there are, and how relatively few 'we' and 'our' hymns there are, which are really suitable for congregational singing. Most of our hymns would be more suitable as solos! It is as if most Christians expect to fly solo to heaven with only just a little bit of formation flying from time to time…"
– *Michael Griffiths*[34]

"What is life, if we have not life together?" – *T.S. Eliot*[35]

God's relationships with humanity throughout history have always been expressed corporately – he has sought to engage with *people*, not only persons. That is not to suggest that individualism is wrong: God deals with us as unique individuals, and salvation is a result of personal faith. The Old Testament never waives the responsibility of the individual.

- GOD ASKS ADAM, 'Where are you?' (Gen 3:9). His question extends to every human being that Adam represented.
- CAIN IS SIMILARLY called to account: 'Where is your brother?' (Gen 4:9).
- THE STORY OF Israel begins with a person, Abraham. It continues with individuals such as Barak (Jdg 4:8), Saul (1 Sam 15:12), David (2 Sam 12:1–10), Ahab (1 Kings 21:17ff) and King Ahaz (Isa 7:1–13) who were all personally confronted.

But as individuals we only discover the potential of our being *imago dei*, made in the image of God, as we take our place in community; for this we have been designed by the God who is himself the triune community. There our personal uniqueness finds its God-created context. It's important that we affirm this, because one challenge that muddies matters for us is our need to read the New Testament in the English language, where 'you' (the second person singular) and 'you' (the second person plural) are the same word.

That means that when we read 'you' in the New Testament, we can jump to the conclusion that Scripture is addressing

## God's unmistakable purpose is to have a people of his own.

us specifically as individuals rather than as part of the corporate body; so we read Paul's words to the Ephesians about putting on the armour of God (Eph 6) and his injunctions about desiring the gifts of the Spirit (1 Cor 12, 14) and then interpret those words into our own personal spirituality rather than seeing the broader communal context.

"Of course we must be 'born again' individually; not as orphans, however, but as members of God's congregational family. At the same time we must not rush to the opposite extreme and become so enthusiastic about corporate and congregational applications of Scripture that we neglect, or underemphasise, the necessity of individual faith and a personal walk with Christ. … We need to emphasise the corporate alongside the personal."
– *Michael Griffiths*[36]

"God's concern for communities must not be thought of as second to his concern for individuals (the way our own concern so often shapes up), for in him the two concerns are organically one. Modern Western Christians, who have been conditioned by their culture to wear the blinkers of a rationalistic individualism, and who are constantly being deafened by the clamour of humanists, for whom society's whole purpose is to extend the individual's range of choices, may find the unity of God's concern for the-individual-in-community and the-community-of-individuals hard to see. But that is our problem. Other generations could see it, and in Scripture the matter is clear."  – *Jim Packer*

"The congregation is the hermeneutic of the gospel."  – *Lesslie Newbigin*[37]

A brief overview shows the **corporate** nature of God's engagement with humanity:

- ADAM AND EVE find their fulfilment together – it was 'not good' for Adam to be alone (Gen 2:18).
- COVENANTS WITH NOAH (Gen 9:8) and Abraham (Gen 12:1, 15:1, 28:14) extend to their descendants and all the families of the earth.
- ISRAEL IS OFTEN simply called 'the people' or 'the people of Yahweh' (Jdg 5:2, 21:2, 15; 1 Sam 4:4, 14:45).
- MANY OLD TESTAMENT laws, including the Ten Commandments, are framed in the second person singular, addressing the individual. But they are addressed to the individual who is not only part of a community but whose individual response is a factor in the moral and spiritual health of that wider community.
- THE OLD TESTAMENT carries the ongoing hope of a Messiah, and a Messiah without a Messianic *people* was unthinkable.[38]
- IN THE VARIOUS annunciations of the birth of Jesus, the angels who appear to Joseph, Zechariah, Simeon and the shepherds all speak of 'his people'. John the Baptist will make ready for the Lord 'a people prepared' (Luke 1:17) and will give knowledge of salvation to 'his people' (Luke 1:68, 77), a light of revelation that will even affect the Gentiles (Luke 2:10, 31, 32), a reminder yet again of the all-inclusive nature of God's mission plan.

- JESUS GATHERS TWELVE disciples – a symbol that points to the formation of a new people of God, a new Israel.
- THE STRONG SENSE of the communal is demonstrated by the plural nouns of the New Testament – brethren (a gender neutral term), children, saints, disciples – and the collective nouns such as flock, nation, people.
- PETER MAKES GREAT use of the theme of 'God's people' in his first letter, quoting verses from Exodus and Deuteronomy (Exod 19:5–6, Deut 7:6) which were originally attributed to Israel and now refer to the new people of God, those who are 'in Christ'. Peter also quotes Hosea 2:23: "I will show my love to the one I called 'Not my loved one'. I will say to those called 'Not my people,' 'You are my people'; and they will say, 'You are my God.'" in 1 Peter 2:10.
- PAUL ECHOES THOSE same scriptures as he speaks of 'God's purpose to purify for himself a people of his own' (Titus 2:14) and also echoes the Hosea text in Romans 9:25. Paul picks up the terms and theme of the old covenant (Jer 31:31ff) and reapplies them to the people of the new covenant, the redeemed people of God (2 Cor 6:16).
- GOD'S HEARTBEAT is described in Exodus: 'I will take you for my people, and I will be your God' (Exod 6:7), and in the closing chapters of Revelation that dream is fulfilled as the new Jerusalem comes down out of heaven, and a voice is heard saying, 'They will be his people, and God himself will be with them and be their God' (Rev 21:3).

"It is … God's unmistakable purpose to have a people of his own, and by his amazing grace it is the utterly undeserved privilege of all who belong to Christ to belong to this community, the people of God."  – *Alan Stibbs*[39]

As we've seen, the Old Testament first reveals that called-out, summoned-for-purpose community as Israel. To them we now turn.

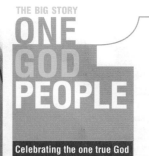

## Teaching Block 2:

# Israel, People for all Peoples: Election's Purpose, Continuity and Optimism

### Election's purpose: Israel and the nations

The turbulent chaos of the Middle East and Israel's central role in that continuing tension surely prompts an awkward question. **Was the isolating of Israel as a chosen people, with their sense of a mandate from God Almighty for their existence and their 'holy land' claims, such a good idea in the first place? Wasn't this an act of favouritism on God's part, and religious justification for elitism and racial superiority?**

We need clear thinking about the purpose and election of Israel. And we must surely challenge unthinking Christian Zionism, and unquestioning support for Israel. Some would say the land of Israel and the Temple no longer have any significance in God's prophetic calendar as these symbols were transfigured by the work of Christ, and those who continue to value the nation-state of Israel deny the full significance of what Christ has done.

Israel was called to be a people – a 'kingdom' (Exod 19:3–6) of priests, prophets and politicians who would profoundly affect the nations of the earth. **They would be a prophetic event that provoked curiosity, and a means of salvation to those who sought it. Their history was written for the sake of the whole of history.** As Chris Wright says, 'God called and chose Israel, not at the expense of the rest, but for the sake of the rest.'[40]

"Right from (Israel's) establishment… at Sinai, there was an awareness that they existed to bring blessing and redemption to humankind (cf. Psa 67, Jer 4:2). Even their national history of redemption was 'made available' to the rest of the nations in the eschatological vision of the Psalms which celebrate the universal kingship of the God of Israel." (Psa 47:1–4,9; 98:1–4, 99:1–4)
– *Chris Wright*[41]

• ISRAEL WAS SPECIFICALLY **called by and for God**. God's people have always been thought of as belonging to him, being God's own possession (Exod 19:5; Deut 7:6; 14:2, 26:18, 1 Peter 2:9 Titus 2:14). This language of election for *purpose* is echoed in the New Testament: It says we are 'called according to his purpose' (Rom 8:28). We should remember this vital truth when we are considering the strengths and weaknesses of the people of God in history, and especially the church today. **The church is God's idea, created by his divine election (Deut 4:32–34). She is his bride**, a concept rooted in Old Testament thinking regarding Israel and obviously developed in New Testament thought about the 'bride of Christ' (Eph 5:23–27). Isaiah (Isa 62:5), Hosea (2:16,19,20) and Ezekiel all allude to this marital relationship between God and Israel. Consider the bitter-sweet words of God, the spurned bridegroom, in Ezekiel 16.

# 2 ONE PEOPLE: IN THE PENTATEUCH

"Later I passed by, and when I looked at you and saw that you were old enough for love, I spread the corner of my garment over you and covered your nakedness. I gave you my solemn oath and entered into a covenant with you, declares the Sovereign Lord, and you became mine. I bathed you with water and washed the blood from you and put ointments on you. I clothed you with an embroidered dress and put leather sandals on you. I dressed you in fine linen and covered you with costly garments. I adorned you with jewellery: I put bracelets on your arms and a necklace around your neck, and I put a ring on your nose, ear-rings on your ears and a beautiful crown on your head. So you were adorned with gold and silver; your clothes were of fine linen and costly fabric and embroidered cloth. Your food was fine flour, honey and olive oil. You became very beautiful and rose to be a queen. And your fame spread among the nations on account of your beauty, because the splendour I had given you made your beauty perfect, declares the Sovereign Lord."

*– Ezekiel 16:8–14*

The church belongs to God: she is his. We must remember this in all of our deliberations about her, lest we fall into the delusion that the church belongs to us.

- **ISRAEL WAS UNIQUE, with religious distinctiveness** (Exod 23:24), in that the people were commanded by God to absolutely reject all other gods. But they were also to be distinctive in their ethics – theirs was a call beyond private piety into a radical lifestyle which had social, economic and political implications. For example, they were called to reject a 'top down' culture of power held by a few; they were instead a tribal society and were more egalitarian than hierarchical, which was a stark contrast to the customs in Canaan where all land was owned by the king. Israel practised multiple ownership by extended families, a system designed to protect the poor (Isa 1:13–17, 1 Kings 22, Micah 3).

- **A CHOSEN PEOPLE AND not a master race.** Israel is usually referred to in the Old Testament as God's *am* – a word that describes a community – rather than his *gôy* – a word for a nation in a geo-political sense. Israel was not a racially 'pure' people. Two tribes (Manasseh and Ephraim) were descended from Joseph's Egyptian wife (Gen 41:50–52), and there were a number of other elements too in her makeup (Exod 12:38, Lev 24:10, Ezek 16:3). **The Old Testament offers no support for ethnic purity or nationalistic superiority, as Israel was formed solely as a result of God's grace. Election offers no opportunity for swaggering or pride** (Deut 7:6–8, 9:4–6, Amos 9:7).

- **INVITED TO THE incredible privilege of being a 'nation of priests'.** In the remarkable statement that Israel would be 'a kingdom of priests and a holy nation' (Exod 19:5ff), God called them to function in a priestly capacity to the global community. In Old Testament practice the priest stood as mediator between God and humanity, and presented the character of God to the people and functioned especially as a teacher (Deut 33:10, Hosea 4:6, Mal 2:4–7). As God was known to the people of Israel through the priesthood, so he would be made known to the world through Israel. One example of that priestly ministry is Abraham's persistent intercession on behalf of Sodom (Gen 18:16ff). And Jeremiah wrote to the exiles in Babylon and urged them to pray for *shalom* (peace) for their oppressors, which was surely far more than a pragmatic policy for survival:

"Also, seek the peace and prosperity of the city to which I have carried you into exile. Pray to the Lord for it, because if it prospers, you too will prosper."

*– Jeremiah 29:7*

- **CALLED TO A prophetic ministry beyond Israel.** Sadly, one of the best examples of an Israelite prophet ministering to a 'foreign' nation is the fugitive Jonah, who went to Nineveh with a rant against God (Jonah 4:1–3). The Assyrians who lived there have been described by historians as the Nazi storm troopers of their day, and patriotic Jonah probably feared that mercy shown to them would signal judgement for his beloved Israel. None the less, we see a Hebrew prophet bringing the word of the Lord to what was not only a pagan nation but an arch-enemy of Israel. It is also the occasion of

**One** Holy, Catholic, Apostolic People

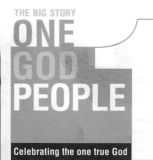

the most successful sermon in the Old Testament – one sentence uttered, and a whole city turns to Yahweh (Jonah 3:4–5).

- **A CATALYST FOR THE development of prophetic politicians**. Such as Joseph and Daniel, who served respectively in Egypt and Babylon, the two nations most identified as the crushing power blocks and oppressors of Israel (Gen 41:41–46, Dan 2:48ff). Both men were able to serve the interests of the states that employed them, were severely tested, sustained by the presence of God, and were able to benefit their own people because of their power and influence. Moses was thoroughly grounded in the thinking and practices of the Egyptian imperial court, so when he was called to confront that power base, he did so with knowledge and understanding.

- **THE CATALYST FOR the hope of all nations being brought under the New Jerusalem of God's reign**, expressed in Isaiah 60, Zechariah 14:16ff, Haggai 2: 6–8, and Isaiah 23:18. The hope is always that the kings of the earth will bring their splendour into the new Jerusalem (Rev 11:15, 21:24). **Breathtakingly, even Egypt and Assyria can have a part, and be on equal terms with Israel, if they will repent and turn to God (Isa 19).**

- **CALLED TO BE a 'church'** – The church of God is the *ekklesia*, a Greek word accurately translated by Tyndale into the English word 'congregation'. In the first century this word was used to describe any regular gathering for any purpose.[42] (Tyndale's good word was sadly replaced in the King James Version by the word 'church' – a poor translation that has led to so much westernized thinking that confuses the church with church buildings.) The Septuagint (the ancient Greek version of the Old Testament) uses the word *ekklesia* to describe the congregation that was Israel, the people summoned together to meet God and to go where God was going (Deut 4:10, 9:10, 18:16, 31:30, Jdg 20:2). **Our word 'church' implies something static and somewhat immovable: the Old Testament ekklesia was a dynamic group, on the move with the Lord at their helm, 'the assembly in the desert' as Stephen described them (Acts 7:38).**

## Election's continuity: we are chosen people too

We are a people elected and chosen by God; the covenantal truth of election is birthed in the Old Testament (Exod 6:7) and developed in the New. Jim Packer's conviction is that Israel's place in history has now been taken by the church.

"**The New Testament announces the extension of God's covenant-promises to the Gentile world and the transference of covenant-privileges from the lineal seed of Abraham to a predominantly Gentile body (cf. Matt 21:43) consisting of all who had become Abraham's true seed and God's true Israel through faith in Christ (Rom 4:9–18; 9:6f.; Gal 3:14ff., 29; 6:16; Eph 2:11ff.; 3:6–8). The unbelieving natural branches were broken off from God's olive tree (the elect community, sprung from the Patriarchs), and wild olive branches (believing Gentiles) were engrafted in their place (Rom 11:16–24). Faithless Israel was rejected and judged, and the international Christian church took Israel's place as God's chosen nation, living in the world as his people and worshipping and proclaiming him as their God.**"

– *Jim Packer*

**However, there are a number of different views about Israel's significance today.** Historically there have been two main theories regarding the church's relationship to Israel.

- IN SUPERCESSIONISM OR replacement theology, the church replaces Israel such that Israel has no redemptive future in any more accelerated way than any other nation.

- IN SEPARATION THEOLOGY, while God has a future for Israel there is a distinction between Israel and the church that is preserved throughout all time with no overlap of the two.

We can highlight a number of parallels and certainties.

- JUST AS ISRAEL was a community called together, so we are 'elected to community and for community'.[43]

- ISRAEL'S ELECTION WAS an act of grace – so now we are elected only 'in Christ' (Eph 1:11).
- JUST AS ISRAEL was chosen for a purpose beyond herself (Gen 12:3) so we are elected to be the people of God for the whole world (Matt 28:16-20). We are 'chosen' to participate in God's programme in history.
- WE ARE 'CIRCUMCISED in heart' (Rom 2:29), the offspring of Abraham (Rom 4:16) and now citizens of God's household (Eph 2:12, 19). God's elective purposes continue.

## Election, hope and pessimism: lighthouse or lifeboat?

❝People are looking for a reason for hope. And I am convinced that the people of God have no higher calling than to offer hope to the world. The only problem is that we cannot offer what we do not possess.❞
                                                        – *Tom Sine*[44]

Matt Redman has expressed in song a question that we must ask.

Can a nation be changed?
Can a nation be saved?
Can a nation be turned back to you?[45]

The strategy that was, and is, election answers this question with an emphatic 'yes'. God's response to the confusion of Babel was optimistic. **The election of Israel as a catalyst of change and reordering for the wider world implies a basic conviction the world *can* be changed. That must not lead us to the idea that our nations are elected in the same way as Israel was; that is not the point. But Israel as a catalyst for change points to the fact that the world *can* be changed.**

God's optimism burned deeply in the hearts of the early pioneers of the modern missionary movement; people such as William Carey, founder of the Baptist Missionary Society (BMS) in the 1790s. Mission activity is married to hope. Visitors to Carey's shoemaker's workshop would discover 'a map of the world, with sheets of paper pasted together,

besmeared with shoemakers wax, and the moral state of every nation depicted with his pen.'[46] Carey was convinced that the world could be transformed by the gospel, that God had 'repeatedly made known his intention to prevail finally over all the power of the devil… and to set up his kingdom among men, and extend it as universally as Satan had extended his.'

David Smith describes the optimism of eighteenth-century evangelicals.

❝They possessed an inexhaustible confidence in the power and grace of God and believed that they stood on the brink of a time when the gospel of Christ was destined to renew and transform the whole of the earth.❞[47]

Isaac Watt's classic hymn sums up that great expectation.

Jesus shall reign where'er the sun
Doth his successive journeys run;
His kingdom stretch from shore to shore,
Till moons shall wax and wane no more

Carey was no mere dreamer. He was hopeful, hard-working, sacrificial and a strategic thinker. In 1793, with one of his sons seriously ill, he wrote:

❝I had fully intended to devote my eldest son to the study of Sanskrit, my second to Persian, and my third to Chinese… . If God should hereafter bless them with his grace, this may fit them for a mission in any part of Persia, India or China.❞[48]

He and his colleagues worked hard to present the gospel in a way that was culturally relevant; in the face of great difficulty, missionaries stuck to their task with amazing faithfulness. Some signed covenants annually that contained these words, 'Let us give ourselves up unreservedly to this glorious cause. Let us never think that our time, our gifts, our strength, our families, or even the clothes we wear, are our own.'

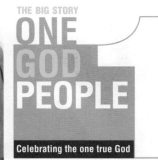

**That hopefulness survived well into the nineteenth century**: renowned Baptist preacher Charles Haddon Spurgeon told the BMS annual meeting in 1858 that the gospel would one day so transform society that war would be a memory: 'When the gospel has its day, wars must cease to the ends of the earth.' But there were voices of disagreement. Growing numbers insisted that the Bible pointed not to the transformation and improvement of the world, but to its inevitable decay and destruction. J.N. Darby, founder of the Plymouth Brethren, was highly vocal in declaring this. Teaching in Geneva in 1840, he poured scorn on the idea of Christian missions leading to the 'progress of good' in the world. **Now the 'lighthouse' model of an elect people influencing the world for God and good was turning into a 'lifeboat' model**, with evangelist D.L. Moody describing the world as a 'wrecked vessel' and insisting that God had given him a lifeboat to save all he could.

By the late nineteenth century, many evangelicals 'seemed to be in retreat before the forces of the modern world,'[49] a beleaguered, stranded people, powerless to do anything much other than grimly 'hold on for dear life' until the Second Coming of Christ. Watt's optimism was replaced by the survivalist, hang-in-there sentiments expressed by Phillip Bliss in his now-infamous hymn, which portrays a struggling church frantically fighting for life, holed up in a fort and almost overwhelmed.

> Ho, my comrades! See the signal waving in the sky!
> Reinforcements now appearing, victory is nigh.
> "Hold the fort, for I am coming," Jesus signals still;
> Wave the answer back to heaven, "By thy grace we will."

**Perhaps we need to recover from a two-hundred-year hangover of pessimism.** The Christian faith provides an antidote for the pessimism and the transitory nature of contemporary culture. We have a world-changing message; in a world that worships the orgasm as 'one of the few contemporary routes to self-transcendence,'[50] we have the Song of Songs, a message to a culture that has forgotten the wonder of pure eroticism. In an age of meaninglessness, we carry the book of Ecclesiastes. In a world of Auschwitz, 9/11,

7/7 and the carnage of Iraq, we turn to Job. When people wrestle with the idea of God, we have the Psalms; and when Make Poverty History, Live 8 and Stop the Traffik cry out on behalf of the oppressed everywhere, we realize that they echo the heartbeat of the Hebrew prophets in their sobs from God's just heart.

Consider the hopeful words of African theologian John Mbiti.

> **"Have we not enough musical instruments to raise the thunderous sound of the glory of God even unto the heaven of heavens? Have we not enough mouths to sing the rhythms of the gospel in our tunes until it settles in our bloodstream? Have we not enough hearts in this continent to contemplate the marvels of the Christian faith? Have we not enough intellectuals in this continent to reflect and theologize on the meaning of the gospel? Have we not enough feet on this continent, to carry the gospel to very corner of this globe?"**
> – *John Mbiti*[51]

> ## A kingdom of justice and righteousness has begun, and is making its way into people's lives.

**What of us in the UK? Do we still have hope for change?**

Melba Padilla Maggay was at the forefront of evangelical involvement in the 'people power' revolution in the Philippines that toppled the unjust Marcos regime. She has navigated through huge disappointments, and describes the tendency of us all, even in our desire to bring change, to 'move towards the dark underside.... Scripture has an ancient name for this: sin.'[52] Yet she remains convinced

## So what? Person to Person: For individual reflection

### Hope eroded through dark propaganda:

In *The Screwtape Letters*, C.S. Lewis describes a dark strategy to 'help' us focus on the more negative traits of the people of God. Uncle Screwtape writes to Wormwood.

"All your patient sees is the half-finished, sham Gothic erection on the new building estate. When he goes inside, he sees the local grocer with rather an oily expression on his face bustling up to offer him one shiny little book containing a liturgy which neither of them understands, and one shabby little book containing corrupt texts of lyrics, mostly bad, and in very small print. When he gets to his pew and looks around him he sees just that selection of his neighbours which he has hitherto avoided. You want to lean heavily on those neighbours. Make his mind flit to and fro between an expression like 'the body of Christ' and the actual faces in the next pew. It matters very little, of course, what kind of people that next pew really contains. You may know one of them to be a great warrior on the Enemy's side. No matter. Your patient, thanks to our father below, is a fool. Provided that any of those neighbours sing out of tune, or have boots that squeak, or double chins, or odd clothes, the patient will quite easily believe that their religion must therefore be somehow ridiculous. At this present stage, you see, he has an idea of 'Christians' in his mind which he supposes to be spiritual but which, in fact, is largely pictorial. His mind is full of togas and sandals and armour and bare legs, and the mere fact that the other people in church wear modern clothes is a real – though of course an unconscious – difficulty to him. Never let it come to the surface; never let him ask what he expected them to look like."[54]

**Israel was called because God graciously loved her, made plans for her, and rescued her.** She was his bride, and her election solely his idea. Do you jump too quickly to criticize or even dismiss the church? Do you focus on her negatives, and develop unrealistic expectations about her?

## So what? Small Groups: For discussion together

**Choose one topic for discussion:**

### Lighthouse under a bushel?

• ISRAEL WAS DESIGNED to be a visible community, a noticeable, provocative people. Discuss ways in which your local church is dynamically connected to the wider community, and consider what might be done to make your church more 'visible'. Why do some churches tend to retreat away from the world they are called to serve?

### Hope killers

When it comes to the church, why are some of us like Lucy in the 'Charlie Brown' cartoon?

Lucy: 'The whole trouble with you, Charlie Brown, is that you're you!'

Charlie Brown: 'Well, what in the world can I do about it?'

Lucy: 'I don't pretend to be able to give advice; I merely point out the trouble.'

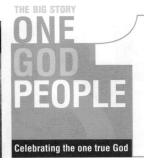

that we can change the world, and calls us to 'practise hope daily' because of 'stubborn grace that shines'.

"So this we believe: a kingdom of justice and righteousness has begun, and it is making its way into people's lives and denting structures that continue to oppress and dehumanise. Such work is seldom done in the corridors of power nor in the halls of the great. Often it is in the many small acts of integrity and goodness that many faceless men and women do every day, believing that behind the face of an evil that is strong is an unseen good that is stronger, even when it wears the face of weakness. It is this daily practice of hope which keeps most of us going, keeping the monsters at bay as humbly and powerfully we are caught up in the kingdom fire and the stubborn grace that shines at the heart of existence." – *Melba Padilla Maggay*[53]

**The people of God are people of calling and hope.**

# One People, called to participate in and rehearse God's story: the power of remembering

It's been said that we tend to forget what we should remember, and we remember what we should forget. Israel was prone to persistent patterns of forgetfulness when it came to the mighty acts of God, with serious and tragic consequences.

## Israel and amnesia

The book of Deuteronomy devotes a third of its text to sustained historical reminders about what God has done. Chapter 8 laments Israel's tendency towards spiritual and historical amnesia, particularly in times of prosperity (Prov 30:7-9) when the need for dependency upon God was lessened.

- REMEMBER HOW THE Lord your God led you all the way in the desert these forty years, to humble you and to test you in order to know what was in your heart, whether or not you would keep his commands (Deut 8:2).
- BE CAREFUL THAT you *do not forget* the Lord your God, failing to observe his commands, his laws and his decrees that I am giving you this day (8:11).
- … THEN YOUR HEART will become proud and *you will forget* the Lord your God, who brought you out of Egypt, out of the land of slavery (8:14).

**Israel enjoyed a breathtaking calling, and an invitation to participate in the greatest storyline of them all. Sadly,**

**she too often preferred selfish subplots that led her into religious idolatry, sexual immorality and consequent judgement, with the surviving people of God wandering around in endless circles in the desert while the promise of the land was held in covenantal suspense.**

Scripture encourages us to learn lessons from the mistakes of our ancestors.

"For I do not want you to be ignorant of the fact, brothers, that our forefathers were all under the cloud and that they all passed through the sea. They were all baptized into Moses in the cloud and in the sea. They all ate the same spiritual food and drank the same spiritual drink; for they drank from the spiritual rock that accompanied them, and that rock was Christ. Nevertheless, God was not pleased with most of them; their bodies were scattered over the desert. Now these things occurred as examples to keep us from setting our hearts on evil things as they did. Do not be idolaters, as some of them were; as it is written: 'The people sat down to eat and drink and got up to indulge in pagan revelry.' We should not commit sexual immorality, as some of them did—and in one day twenty-three thousand of them died. We should not test the Lord, as some of them did—and were killed by snakes. And do not grumble, as some of them did—and were killed by the destroying angel. These things happened to them as examples and were written down as warnings for us, on whom the fulfilment of the ages has come. So, if you think you are standing firm, be careful that you don't fall!"
— *1 Corinthians 10:1–12*

The deliverance from Egypt in the Exodus and the giving of the law at Mount Sinai were the pivotal points of the story, rooting Israel in the *intervention* of God in history and the *revelation* of God in the giving of the law. We can be tempted to view the law in somewhat oppressive and negative terms, because we rush to celebrate that in Christ we are 'not under the law' (Rom 3:19, 6:14). But God had lovingly redeemed his people and called them to a new

life in and through him; now the law set out the context of what that life should look like.

"We need to remind ourselves that the ancient Israelites looked on the law not as a burden but as a gift of grace, a delight, precisely because of the relationship with God that it enabled and expressed." — *Chris Wright*[55]

The Decalogue (the ten 'words' or commandments) was at the heart of Israelite life, as statements that were self-contained and final, given by God himself. It provided Israel with direction on the broadest range of issues, including criminal, civil, family, cultic and charitable law.

"[The Decalogue] stood in association with the review of the Sinai events as the binding charter expressing the will of the divine Lord of the Covenant." — *J.J. Stamm*[56]

Again, the wisdom of the law was part of the 'lighthouse effect' that was supposed to emanate from Israel. **The law was given to Israel by their God, who was and is also Sovereign Lord of the universe and so is Lord of all – and thus his law has moral implications for all. The intention was that other nations would see the marvellous order that Israel enjoyed, and be prompted to ask questions about the source of their wisdom, the God of Israel.**

"See, I have taught you decrees and laws as the Lord my God commanded me, so that you may follow them in the land you are entering to take possession of it. Observe them carefully, for this will show your wisdom and understanding to the nations, who will hear about all these decrees and say, 'Surely this great nation is a wise and understanding people.' What other nation is so great as to have their gods near them the way the Lord our God is near us whenever we pray to him? And what other nation is so great as to have such righteous decrees and laws as this body of laws I am setting before you today?" — *Deuteronomy 4:5–8*

**If God's people, Israel, were to faithfully be the people of the Big Story, the principles of the law had to be**

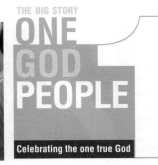
communicated creatively, passionately and in as many different expressions as possible to counteract the 'amnesia' they were so prone to.

**We face the same challenge, because we can suffer from similar memory lapses.** In 1975 Michael Griffiths, then General Director of the Overseas Missionary Fellowship, wrote a pithy and prophetic book with a telling title: *Cinderella with Amnesia*.

"Christians collectively seem to be suffering from a strange amnesia. A high proportion of people who 'go to church' have forgotten what it is all for. Week by week they attend services in a special building and go through their particular, time honoured routine, but give little thought to the purpose of what they are doing."
 – *Michael Griffiths*[57]

The people of God are only able to fulfil their prophetic calling as long as they imbibe, rehearse and live out God's story; without that story, they are like 'salt that has lost its saltiness' (Matt 5:13). When the dreaded amnesia sets in, the people of God become functionally useless, or as Jesus put it more plainly, 'no longer good for anything.' Then the world, now denied the antiseptic, cleansing power of the salt-people, descends into greater rot and decay. The corporate memory needs vivid and creative jogs. Here's the challenge. Are we boring? Do we neglect some clear biblical injunctions and examples towards creativity, thus turning faith into something tedious?

## Creativity, surgery and gathering

**God 'the great dramatist' used a vast number of props in order to continually instil the big story into Israel's consciousness.** Israel experienced the story with her taste buds as she ate unleavened bread to celebrate the Passover (Exod 12:17–20). She scribbled the story on the doorposts of her houses; she wore the story, tying its symbols on her hands and foreheads (Deut 6:8–9). She sang and danced the story (Exod 15:20–21), and preserved some of her miracle 'manna' in a jar 'for the generations to come'.

"'The Word became flesh,' St. John said. And the church has turned flesh back into words." – *Tom Wright*[58]

"Perhaps the special character of the stories… lies in the fact that they are not told for themselves, that they are not only about other people, but that they are always about us. They locate us in the very midst of the great story and plot of all time and space, and therefore relate us to the great dramatist and story teller, God himself." – *John Dunne*[59]

**In Israel, the story was to be gossiped in everyday life, not just expressed in formalized religious ceremonies. Rather, Israel was called to rehearse the script continually – at home, on the road and when resting or active.** The story was immortalized by commemoration, as altars and stone pillars were built to mark the spots of historic triumphs (Exod 17:15, Deut 27:4). Words were accompanied by rich and vivid symbols; Israelites had blood splashed over them as Moses read them the law (Exod 24:8).

The story was constructed by builders and curtain makers in the development of the tabernacle and temple. Furniture makers carved the story in wood (Exod 25:10–16), sculptors sculpted it and metalworkers hammered it out (Exod 25:18), and jewellers set the story in precious stones (Exod 28:17). The story was smelled as incense was offered, it was acted out through the elaborate sacrificial system, it was chimed as the priestly bells sounded.

The priests, with their colourful vestments, were lead players in the drama; the breastplate, turban, sash and ephod enabled the embroiderers to stitch the story (Exod 28:39).

But the drama went further, cutting into Israel's time – and flesh – in the creation of the festivals and feasts, and the rite of circumcision.

Elderly Abraham, ninety-nine years old, was circumcised on the same day as Ishmael, who was thirteen years old (Gen 17:24–27). Circumcision was the sign of covenant, the reminder of a union with God that made its mark at the very depths of the human psyche, even beyond gender, faith impacting that which is most private and usually hidden. During the later journey through the wilderness, the practice of circumcision fell into disuse, but was resumed by the command of Joshua before they entered the Promised Land (Josh 5:2–9).

> "This is my covenant with you and your descendants after you, the covenant you are to keep: Every male among you shall be circumcised. You are to undergo circumcision, and it will be the sign of the covenant between me and you."
> – Genesis 17:10–11

Circumcision was a symbol of purity (Isa 52:1). The Old Testament speaks of uncircumcised lips (Exod 6:12, 30), ears (Jer 6:10) and hearts (Lev 26:41). Even the fruit of a tree that is unclean is spoken of as uncircumcised (Lev 19:23). But primarily it was a very real reminder to the bearer of the mark that they were different. It said, You belong to God.

**Israel was also called to prioritize the covenantal celebrations**, the sacred assemblies (Lev 23:2) of Passover, tabernacles, first fruits, weeks and trumpets – and Sabbath. There was sense of party and inter-tribal unification in these events – hence the radical *command* of Deuteronomy 14:26.

> "Use the silver to buy whatever you like: cattle, sheep, wine or other fermented drink or anything you wish. Then you and your household shall eat there in the presence of the Lord your God, and rejoice."

But there was obviously a far deeper purpose, as God's people gathered together to remember and give thanks.

> "We can find no period in Israel's history when she did not believe she was the chosen people of Yahweh. … The prophets and the writers continually harped back to the Exodus as the unforgettable example of the power and grace of Yahweh, calling the people to himself. It is clear that from earliest times Israel saw

herself as a people chosen by Yahweh and the object of his special favour."
> – John Bright[60]

**The festivals and gatherings were also opportunities for covenant renewal, evaluation and definition.** The Old Testament celebrations enabled the people of God to question themselves: Had they been faithful to the covenant? Where had they failed? Had they been faithful to the story?

**The festival enabled the people to quite literally re-enact their history creatively.** They would not just hear the story rehearsed in words, but would participate as players in a huge play where they were the actors and audience both. The Passover feast was to be eaten by a people dressed and ready for a journey, with cloaks tucked into belts, sandals on the feet and a staff in hand (Exod 12:11). A mass campout lasting seven days was required when the Feast of the Tabernacles was celebrated (Lev 23:42). **It was not enough to hear the story of the nomadic journeying of their ancestors through the wilderness; the people had to live in booths made of tree boughs and the branches of palm trees for seven days, to feel and experience something of what their predecessors had experienced.**

Ben Patterson tells a story about Rabbi Abraham Heschel that illustrates the power of the truth dramatized.

> "Some of the members of the synagogue told him that the liturgy did not express what they felt. Would he please change it? Heschel wisely told them that it was not for the liturgy to express what they felt, it was for them to learn to feel what the liturgy expressed. As Jews they were to learn the drama and say it and 'play' it over and over again until it captured their imagination and they assimilated it into the deepest places in their hearts. Then, and only then, would it be possible for them to live properly their own individual dramas."[61]

> "Metaphor, symbol, ritual, sign and myth, long maligned by those only interested in 'exact' expressions of rationality, are today being rehabilitated; they not only

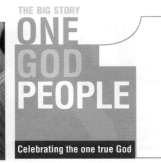
"touch the mind and its conceptions, and evoke action with a purpose, but compel the heart." – *David Bosch*[62]

"What a story does is sneak up behind you and whisper something in your ear, and when you turn round to see what it is, it kicks you in the butt and runs and hides behind a bush." – *Brian McLaren*[63]

And the story was for all – young and old alike.

## Let me tell you a story: the big story for little ones

"It is through hearing stories about wicked stepmothers, lost children, good but misguided kings, and youngest sons who receive no inheritance but must make their own way in the world that children learn or mislearn both what a child and what a parent is, what the cast of characters may be in the drama into which they have been born and what the ways of the world are. Deprive children of stories and you leave them unscripted, anxious stutterers as much in their actions as in their words. Hence there is no way to give us an understanding of any society, including our own, except through the stock of stories which constitute its initial dramatic resources." – *Alasdair MacIntyre*[64]

In the Pentateuch there is an insistence that the story be passed on from generation to generation. The primary responsibility for the passing on the story to children was given to their parents, not the priests. Not only was the possibility of meaningful question and answer within family units assumed, but actively encouraged and provided for.

"These commandments that I give you today are to be upon your hearts. Impress them on your children. Talk about them when you sit at home and when you walk along the road, when you lie down and when you get up. Tie them as symbols on your hands and bind them on your foreheads. Write them on the doorframes of your houses and on your gates." – *Deuteronomy 6:6–9*

"When you enter the land that the Lord will give you as he promised, observe this ceremony. And when your children ask you, 'What does this ceremony mean to you?' then tell them, 'It is the Passover sacrifice to the Lord, who passed over the houses of the Israelites in Egypt and spared our homes when he struck down the Egyptians.' Then the people bowed down and worshiped." – *Exodus 12:25–28*

"In the future, when your son asks you, 'What is the meaning of the stipulations, decrees and laws the Lord our God has commanded you?' tell him: 'We were slaves of Pharaoh in Egypt, but the Lord brought us out of Egypt with a mighty hand. Before our eyes the Lord sent miraculous signs and wonders—great and terrible—upon Egypt and Pharaoh and his whole household. But he brought us out from there to bring us in and give us the land that he promised on oath to our forefathers. The Lord commanded us to obey all these decrees and to fear the Lord our God, so that we might always prosper and be kept alive, as is the case today. And if we are careful to obey all this law before the Lord our God, as he has commanded us, that will be our righteousness." – *Deuteronomy 6:20–25*

If we are to have any hope of reaching children and young people, then we must help connect them to the Big Story. Jim Partridge, a local church leader and youth specialist, has first-hand experience of this.

"Increasingly when I am working with young people outside of the church, I need to explain to them the big picture of the Bible. They have no concept of sin without understanding creation; the only way to fully understand suffering is to know that all creation is waiting and groaning; you can't fully explain the cross without explaining the sacrificial system of the Old Testament: and so it goes on.

"I am increasingly finding the need in outreach and discipleship to explain the big story of who we are and about the origins of the world they live in. Now, when we get onto discussing 'one people' I get so excited, because I don't think we often teach what it means to be the people of God. In the sense of, we don't paint the big picture that the Bible portrays. So a young person's perception of church is often of a service they go to once a week and a community they kind of exist in but it seems quite removed from their real communities amongst their peers or at school/college. In this sense they have a limited vision for the people of God 'to fill the earth and subdue it'. They have no understanding that it is God's intention that through the church his manifold wisdom will be made known to the heavenly realms. They don't understand what it means to be the bride of Christ. They don't realise that they, made in the image of God, are the people who reflect who God is; that we are like art on display in a gallery, you only know the artist and what the artist is like by looking at the painting. That God is into making new creations in the sense of finding these pieces of art covered over with dust sheets, with dulled colours and he is into restoring them to become all that they were created to be and on display for the world to see. And we don't make the links for them between Genesis 1 and 2 and Matthew 28. God's original intention was that the earth would be full of worshippers, made in the image of God, to care for his world and be in relationship with him. Therefore how we live our lives matter, because God created us to care for his planet and all that is within it, which is why the use of the world's resources, pollution, poverty, caring for the widow and orphans, all these issues really matter. …

"Young people in general don't understand why having a greater knowledge of our roots (back to Abraham) makes sense of being a called out people on earth. They are generally not taught about what it means to be 'strangers and aliens' in the world and all the amazing descriptions given in 1 Peter 2 about being a nation, a priesthood, a people belonging to God. They are not generally taught about Revelation 21 and the restoration of all things where God himself will be with his people. They don't really understand the old and new covenant and how the heroes of the faith were commended for their faith but that we have received something more amazing and that God has planned something better for us.

"All this has massive implications for our understanding on our self-image and our identity if we know our history, our ancestral roots, our reason for being, our purpose for being here on earth, and our final destination. We can only make sense of our present by understanding our beginning and our ultimate end. I think a greater revelation and understanding of what it means to be the people of God gives young people something to live for. For those frustrated and not engaged in their local church, it helps them grasp a greater feel about what it means to be Christian and what it means to be part of the people of God. I think it helps them in church situations that may not be that enthralling to get stuck in because they see the bigger picture, and their week to week church experience is not the whole deal but part of something much bigger and broader and higher and wider: God's people going to the nations, looking after the planet as he originally intended and pointing all people back to the originator of all things. …

"So an opportunity, like we have at Spring Harvest in 2007, to paint the big picture for people, especially young people, is so exciting."
– *Jim Partridge*[65]

## Lacey's heritage: creativity

Rob Lacey, writer and actor, was well known to Spring Harvest guests and an advisor to the Spring Harvest leadership team. The 2006 event began with a moving and poignant play about suffering, a piece that not only flowed from Rob's pen but from his heart and painful experience as he battled cancer. Some months before his death, the Spring Harvest leadership team travelled together to Rob and Sandra's home in Cardiff, to pray with them and share a meal. **During a moving couple of hours, there was only one moment when Rob shed any tears, which is surprising given the physical and emotional pain he was**

enduring. That moment came when he spoke of the need to safeguard the huge contribution made by creative people in the church; the offerings of the actors, dancers, sculptors, painters, poets and playwrights must absolutely not be marginalized, he said as a tear ran down his cheek. Not only have we as the church often frustrated those who want to express their faith using tools others than words, but we have frequently turned the most epic Big Story that has ever been into a bland, monochrome dirge. We have seen today that far from being a mere fashionable trend, creativity saturates Old Testament faith and flows through the Bible until the final full stop in the apocalyptic imagery of the book of Revelation.

We not only remember Rob with great joy and affection, but we want to heed well his tearful exhortation: Let the church honour, release and value the creative gifts given by her Creator God, and so celebrate and enjoy more of God's stunning creative genius.

## Rob's God
### (for Rob Lacey) by Gerard Kelly

I want to follow Rob's God;
God-the-goal of my soul's education.
Rob's God is approachable, articulate and artful,
A glowing God,
Of graceful inclination.

Rob's God snowboards cloudscapes
And paints daisies on his toes,
While watching Chaplin re-runs on his iPod.
He smiles at cats and children,
Jumps in puddles
With his shoes on,
A 'where's-the-fun-in-fundamentalism?' God.

Rob's God doesn't shoot
His own wounded,
Or blame the poor for failing
At prosperity.
He doesn't beat the broken
With bruised reeds from their garden,
Or tell the sick that healing's their
Responsibility.

Rob's God is a poet,
Painting people as his poems;
A sculptor shaping symphonies from stone
A maker of mosaics
Curator of collages
Woven from the wounds and wonders
We have known

A furnace of forgiveness;
Rob's God radiates reunion
Pouring oil on every fight
We've ever started
A living lover
Loving laughter
Lending light
To the helpless and the harmed and heavy-hearted

Other Gods may claim more crowded churches
Higher profiles
Better ratings
Fuller phone-ins
But in the contest for commitment
In the battle for belief
In the war to woo my worship;
Rob's God wins
In the fight for my faith's fervour:
In the struggle for my soul;
In the race for my respect
Rob's God wins.

Absolutely.

# 2 ONE PEOPLE: IN THE PENTATEUCH

## So what? Person to Person: For individual reflection

### What does being at Spring Harvest mean for you this week?

Consider L. M. Montgomery's words from *Emily of New Moon*:

"It had always seemed to Emily, ever since she could remember that she was very, very near to a world of wonderful beauty. Between it and herself hung only a thin curtain; she could never draw the curtain aside – but sometimes, just for a moment, a wind fluttered it and then it was as if she had caught a glimpse of the enchanting realm beyond – only a glimpse – and heard the note of unearthly music. The moment came rarely – went swiftly, leaving her breathless with the impossible delight of it. She could never recall it – never summon it – never pretend it; but the wonder of it stayed with her for days. It never came twice with the same thing. Tonight the dark boughs against that far off sky had given it. It had come with a wild, high note of wind in the night, with a shadow wave over a

ripe field, with grey bird lighting on her window still in a storm, with the singing of 'Holy! Holy! Holy!' in church, with the glimpse of the kitchen fire when she had come home on a dark autumn night, with the spirit like blue of ice palms on a twilight pane, with a felicitous new word when she was writing down a 'description;' of something. And always when the flash came to her, Emily felt that life was a wonderful, mysterious thing of persistent beauty.[66]

• THERE IS A danger that the Spring Harvest event becomes an exhausting rush. It can turn into a frantic time to gather new ideas that we must implement immediately, a time to compile a list of all of the changes we must make, instead of being an opportunity to celebrate with fellow believers from a huge variety of backgrounds the wonder of what God has done and who we are right now in Christ. Give yourself permission to rest, to think, be thankful and recover the sense of beauty in life, as you reconnect again with the Big Story of God.

**One** Holy, Catholic, Apostolic People

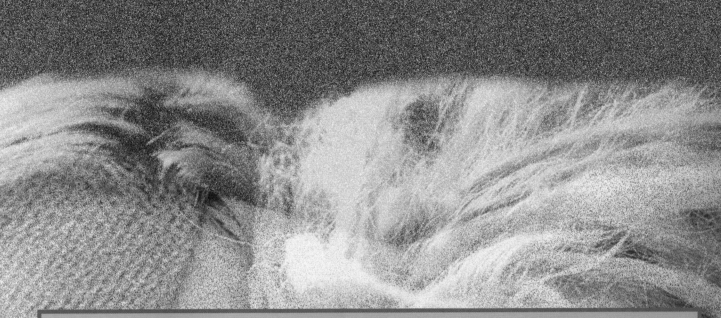

## So what? Small Groups: For discussion together

**Choose one topic for discussion**

- **CREATIVITY CENTRE STAGE.** Creativity is not an element of church life that should be shunted away or treated as a fad, or as a 'nouveau' and possibly suspect aspect of modern church life. We must empower the artists among us, and realize that just as Israel's festivals 'preached' the truth, so our artists and dramatists today do not function as ancillaries to the preacher but are 'preachers' themselves. Just as Israel told herself the story in a huge variety of different ways, so we can do the same. Is that happening in our churches? How?

- **TELLING THE STORY.** How can we recover the ability to tell the story – one generation to another – to children? Can non-parents have a part in this? And if so, how? Perhaps the practice of appointing godparents should be taken more seriously in some quarters of the church as a way of strategically providing for the telling of the story between the generations. Should we create a Christian *bar mitzvah* (for boys) or *bat mitzvah* (for girls) as a rite of passage that celebrates the advent of adulthood in our children that is more age specific than the Anglican act of confirmation?

## Suggested reading

**Remembering our Future – Walker and Bretherton, Paternoster**

A COLLECTION OF WRITINGS by eminent thinkers with a passion for the church. The range and scope of this book provokes the reader to think deeply and serve passionately.

**Preach the Word! – Greg Haslam, SOV**

PREACHING HAS A huge part to play in telling the story of God. Practical hands-on advice from respected preachers and teachers.

# 3 ONE PEOPLE: IN THE PROPHETS

One Holy, Catholic, Apostolic People

As obedient children, do not conform to the evil desires you had when you lived in ignorance. But just as **he who called you is holy, so be holy in all you do; for it is written: 'Be holy, because I am holy'**. – *1 Peter 1:14–16*

"Therefore say to the house of Israel, 'This is what the Sovereign Lord says: It is not for your sake, O house of Israel, that I am going to do these things, but **for the sake of my holy name**, which you have profaned among the nations where you have gone. **I will show the holiness of my great name**, which has been profaned among the nations, the name you have profaned among them. Then the nations will know that I am the Lord, declares the Sovereign Lord, when **I show myself holy through you before their eyes.**"

– *Ezekiel 36:22-23*

# 3 ONE PEOPLE: IN THE PROPHETS

## Teaching Block 1:

### The constant 'middle c': the holy God

Teaching Block 1: Our aim is to understand that the issue of holiness sits at the heart of the nature of God and the nature of the universe we live in, and to realise how far some of our present teaching and understanding of holiness has deviated from the biblical teaching.

We shall come to understand that our life of holiness is rooted in God, whose character is constant, unfathomable, immanent, intimacy and love.

We shall explore this contrast of transcendence and immanence and how it shapes our view of holiness.

We shall explore the idea that holiness is a response rather than a demand and how that practically works out in social engagement.

We shall explore what quality of 'otherness' the people of God should live out and live for.

## Teaching Block 2:

### Distinctive people: holiness snapshots

Teaching Block 2: Our aim is to look at how holiness is the defining mark of the People of God.

We shall consider how this is worked out in the church with particular exploration of how we are to be:

- Distinctive – a chance to rediscover a theocratic radicalism. This is interesting terminology in the present day. What does this look like in the UK today?

And how do we as the People of God permeate the culture and our society with Shalom?

- Transformed – and to be transformers.
- A people of purity – looking for the lost joy of a faith-filled holy life.
- Holy – in a context where the effect of sin has led to the dehumanisation of humanity for all.

## Teaching Block 3:

### Looking closer: shalom, righteousness and justice

Teaching Block 3: Our aim is to explore the imperative for holiness to have an outward expression in the struggle for justice and how this connects with our exploration of Shalom.

We shall consider positive and negative examples (in our history and in the present day) of the church's pursuit – or neglect – of justice issues.

We shall give opportunity for discussion about how the church can help take forward initiatives that are local and national.

# One **Holy** People – the People of God in the Prophets and Histories

# Introduction

## Prelude: The unmasking

"Woe to you, teachers of the law and Pharisees, you hypocrites! You shut the kingdom of heaven in men's faces. You yourselves do not enter, nor will you let those enter who are trying to. Woe to you, teachers of the law and Pharisees, you hypocrites! You travel over land and sea to win a single convert, and when he becomes one, you make him twice as much a son of hell as you are."
– *Matthew 23:13–15*

They were skilled thespians who made audiences gasp, laugh and cry out loud thousands of years before computerized special effects and Hollywood. As the actors plied their craft onstage, their vividly painted, grossly exaggerated masks made them look so convincing. They were called the *hypokrites*, and it's possible that Jesus, as a boy, might have seen them in action – the remains of a theatre have been discovered in the area where he was raised.

**In Jesus' time there were some who used religion as a script for the daily performance, and whose lives were a well-rehearsed, pious masquerade. The street corners were their stage as they prayed loudly, with trembling voices and elaborate vocabulary.** They invested heavily in the wardrobe department, purchasing dress-to-impress gowns and dangling phylacteries – leather bound scriptures tied to their hair. But their fake lives did more than damage themselves; they were taking the wonderful truth of holiness – the call to live a life dedicated to the beautiful, holy God – and turning it into a combination of farce and

tragedy. Jesus chose a popular word to denounce them. He dubbed these gifted pretenders 'hypokrites' – the actual name used to describe those travelling bands of actors in the Greek theatres. *Hypocrites*. Matthew's Gospel describes the dramatic showdown between Jesus and the scribes and Pharisees. Consider this excerpt.

"Woe to you, blind guides! You say, 'If anyone swears by the temple, it means nothing; but if anyone swears by the gold of the temple, he is bound by his oath.' You blind fools! Which is greater: the gold, or the temple that makes the gold sacred? You also say, 'If anyone swears by the altar, it means nothing; but if anyone swears by the gift on it, he is bound by his oath.' You blind men! Which is greater: the gift, or the altar that makes the gift sacred? Therefore, he who swears by the altar swears by it and by everything on it. And he who swears by the temple swears by it and by the one who dwells in it. And he who swears by heaven swears by God's throne and by the one who sits on it. Woe to you, teachers of the law and Pharisees, you hypocrites! You give a tenth of your spices—mint, dill and cummin. But you have neglected the more important matters of the law—justice, mercy and faithfulness. You should have practised the latter, without neglecting the former. You blind guides! You strain out a gnat but swallow a camel."
– *Matthew 23:16–24*

As sermons go, it was about as blunt as they get. One commentator describes Jesus' stinging words as offensive.

# 3 ONE PEOPLE: IN THE PROPHETS

"Jesus goes on the offensive, and offensive is not too strong a word for much of the language that he uses here."

– *R.T. France*[67]

Because of the continuous confrontations between Jesus and these religious leaders, it's too easy to quickly demonise them altogether like pantomime baddies. But the worrying truth is that, **for the most part, these were very good people gone wrong; their intentions were initially noble, but they had become corrupted by the very system of 'holiness' that they had engineered. Holiness had gradually aged from being something fresh and beautiful, into something fearsome, ugly and largely unattainable.**

There were several thousand Pharisees spread throughout Israel in Jesus' day.[68] They longed for the political freedom of Israel, and to see the nation purged of paganism. More a pressure group than office holders, they are described by the Jewish historian Philo,[69] a contemporary of Jesus and Paul, as 'full of zeal for the laws, the strictest guardians of the ancestral traditions.'[70] The Pharisees believed it was more valuable to study the law than engage in temple worship. They wanted to end all divisions between the sacred and the secular, and rightly taught that the whole of life should be lived before God (which ironically was part of their downfall – their desire to see every meal as an act of worship meant that they were unable to share meals with 'sinners', and this brought them into direct conflict with Jesus). Far from being dead traditionalists, they were passionate reformers, insisting that God's presence was not limited to a special building, but as it says in the Mishnah: "If two sit together and study Torah, the Divine Presence rests between them."[71]

**So far, so good – perhaps. The sermon recorded in Matthew 23 came as a response to their utterly false, flawed system of holiness.** The Pharisees were rigidly upholding holiness teaching that:

- WAS ROOTED IN extra-biblical authority – revering what humans called for rather than what God demanded. Many traditions develop holiness codes that are based on history and culture rather than biblical imperatives (Matt 23:2–3).

- WAS TAUGHT BY controlling and manipulative leadership, but not *practised* by them. They were upholding a system that was impossible to maintain, which smothered with guilt those who genuinely wanted to pursue God while the Pharisees in practice exempted themselves (vv3–4).

- WAS A SYSTEM designed to elevate the status and title power of leaders. We saw yesterday that Israel was chosen to call attention to God, and not to herself (vv5–12). As somewhat self-appointed guardians of the law, many of the Pharisees had become arrogant and haughty.

- CREATED A 'SLAMMED door' effect, and kept people away from God, rather than drew them to him (vv13–14).

- APPEARED 'EVANGELISTIC' BUT was actually an efficient machine for turning out dangerously passionate 'converts' such as Saul, who was later to become Paul. Biblical history shows that zealots are often completely misguided (v15, Phil 3:6).

- STARTED ENDLESS TIME-CONSUMING debates on minutiae such as lesser and greater oaths. This internalised nit-picking diverted the people of God from their true mission. Many 'holiness' groups have no time to actually reach out to the world (vv16–22).

- FOCUSED ON TINY pietistic details, but ignored massive injustices like the oppression of the poor, and true justice, mercy and righteousness (vv23–24).

- WAS MORE CONCERNED about keeping up appearances – *looking* right – than with genuine heart purity – *being* right (vv25–28).

- CHERISHED PROUD NOTIONS of superiority in the belief that they had not made the mistakes of others, especially their ancestors (vv29–32).

- FAR FROM BRINGING pleasure and delight to God, mutated 'holiness' into something that invoked his anger and judgement (v33ff).

**These passionate radicals created a bewildering labyrinth that made holy living impossible. As the people of God today, we must avoid their mistakes at all costs.**

One **Holy**, Catholic, Apostolic People

## Holiness: for Bible carriers and binge drinkers

Our journey into holiness is vital. No less than eight times in Scripture, God's call is repeated: 'Be holy, for I am holy'. Ajith Fernando states that of the 2,005 verses in Paul's writings 1,400 have something to day about holiness, godliness or Christian character.[72] But the very word 'holy' is so seldom used these days; and when it is used in our culture, it usually has negative connotations. This can lead us to think that our study today is a somewhat cloistered matter, one to be taken *by* church people and *for* church people. Nothing could be further from the truth.

**The issue of holiness sits at the heart of the nature of God, and the nature of the universe we live in. The call to live in holiness is a summons for all humanity, not just for the religious; the truth about holiness answers the fundamental question of humankind: 'how then should we live?'**

A brief look at the tabloid press shows that we live in a somewhat hopeless moral wilderness; just as in the days of Ecclesiastes, money, sex and drugs provide escape for those who, according to one commentator, 'lack the strength to look death in the face'.

**At a time when binge drinking is an epidemic problem, drug abuse with associated crime issues continues unabated, and credit card debt is astronomical, our journey is vital and relevant.**

"Being unable to cure death, wretchedness and ignorance, men have decided, in order to be happy, not to think about such things."
— *Blaise Pascal*[73]

"Modern man is drinking or drugging himself out of awareness, or shopping, which is the same thing."
— *Ernest Becker*[74]

So today we will:

- Look at the **root, source and reason for holiness – the character of God**; we will consider the temptation to 'revise' him that seems so persistent among the people of God.

- Take a **broad overview of the nature of authentic holiness** as we consider that holiness was being increasingly misunderstood in the time of the Old Testament prophets and histories, leading ultimately to the aberrational thinking of the Pharisees in Jesus' time.

- Consider what **righteousness is, and see that social engagement generally and action on behalf of the poor and marginalized especially sits at the heart not only of the gospel, but the historic call to the people of God**. In this bi-centennial year that celebrates the work of anti-slavery statesman William Wilberforce, we will look at the Stop the Traffik campaign and other current initiatives.

**So much for the details of where we are going today. But how shall we go? What will our attitude be as we travel together?**

## Considering holiness today

**As we spend time together reflecting on the character of our holy God and his clear call for us to live holy lives, we must do more than a scientific examination of the theology of holiness: we come to consider, and therefore surely worship, our beautiful God and ponder the winsome challenge to beautiful living that he places before us.**

In the film *Mr. Holland's Opus*[75], Glenn Holland tries to convince a hesitant clarinettist that she is missing the point of everything. His words must resonate with us as we consider holiness.

"There's a lot more to music than notes on a page. It's about feelings, and moving people, and something beautiful and being alive and having fun."
— *Mr. Holland*

If we are to avoid the sin of the Pharisees, we must realize that holiness is more than law and involves passion – being

# 3 ONE PEOPLE: IN THE PROPHETS

wonderfully alive, and being able to experience the laughter and joy in life that God intended.

As we come in prayer to our holy God, consider the mixture of joy and reverential worship described in Kenneth Grahame's *The Wind in the Willows*[76], although it should be noted that Grahame is not writing in a Christian context – indeed he was probably a pantheist – but what he has to say conveys something of the mystery of an encounter with the divine.

> 'This is the place of my song-dream, the place
> the music played to me', whispered the Rat,
> as if in a trance. 'Here, in this holy place, here
> if anywhere, surely we shall find Him!'
>
> Then suddenly the Mole felt a great Awe fall upon
> him, an awe that turned his muscles to water, bowed
> his head, and rooted his feet to the ground. It was
> no panic terror – indeed he felt wonderfully at peace
> and happy – but it was an awe that smote and held
> him and, without seeing, he knew it could only mean
> that some august Presence was very, very near. …
>
> Perhaps he would never have dared to raise his
> eyes, but that… the call and the summons seemed
> still dominant and imperious. He might not refuse,
> were Death himself not waiting to strike him
> instantly, once he had looked with mortal eye on
> things rightly kept hidden. Trembling he obeyed,
> and raised his humble head; and then… he looked
> in the very eyes of the Friend and Helper… .
>
> 'Rat!' he found breath to whisper,
> shaking. 'Are you afraid?'
>
> 'Afraid?' murmured the Rat, his eyes shining with
> unutterable love. 'Afraid of *Him*? O, never, never!
> And yet – and yet – O, Mole, I am afraid!'

## Pause for Prayer

Awesome God,

You are the holiest of all, and yet you rush to embrace us, still grimy, still sullied by sin.

You are the strongest of all, and yet you stoop to press your hand into our hands, still trembling and weak.

You are the most beautiful of all, and yet you lean towards us in our ugliness with a warm kiss of welcome.

You are the highest of all, but you have come to our deepest darkness in the Cross.

You are the most lovable of all, and yet you decide to love us, so unlovely.

You are who you are, and yet you choose friendship with us, knowing so clearly who we are, what we are, and where we have been.

Holy God, make us like you.

Amen.

One **Holy**, Catholic, Apostolic People

## Teaching Block 1:

# The constant 'middle C' – the Holy God

Lloyd C. Douglas, who wrote the novel *The Robe*, tells of a retired music teacher he met at university. They lived in the same lodgings. The older man was disabled and unable to leave his apartment. A daily ritual of sorts developed between them; every morning, Douglas would open the old man's door and ask the same question: 'Well, what's the good news?' The older gentleman would always pick up his tuning fork, tap it on the metal arm of his wheelchair, and say the same thing.

❝That's middle C! It was middle C yesterday; it will be middle C tomorrow; it will be middle C a thousand years from now. The tenor upstairs sings flat, the piano across the hall is out of tune, but that, my friend, is middle C!❞[77]

**In our confused world, God stands above the post-modern clamour as the one who is the 'middle C', the constant reality upon whom we can depend.**

❝To whom will you compare me, or who is my equal? says the Holy One.❞ – *Isaiah 40:25*

**Throughout her history, Israel was tempted to revise God, to try to make him into what she wanted him to be. The rot set in quickly; even while Moses was up on Mount Sinai receiving the law, the Hebrews became religious consumers.**

Aaron shaped a golden calf, and then a remarkable statement was made about his handiwork.

❝These are your gods, O Israel, who brought you up out of Egypt.❞ – *Exodus 32:4b*

Aaron went on to call 'a festival to the Lord' for the following day. In his thinking, God had truly been honoured. Whenever humanity tries to revise God, not only is doctrinal truth a casualty, but human behaviour degenerates too.

❝So the next day the people rose early and sacrificed burnt offerings and presented fellowship offerings. Afterward they sat down to eat and drink and got up to indulge in revelry.❞ – *Exodus 32:6*

**Instead of responding to the absolute self-revelation of God – the great 'I am' (Exod 20) – the Hebrews shifted into reverse and began to create God according to their own subjective and immediate wish list. Impatient with God's mountain-top conference with Moses, they sought to revise their *God* and unwittingly devised a *god*.**

Karl Barth confronted this tendency to create God according to human speculation. Dismissed by conservatives because of his views on biblical criticism and scorned by liberals as a biblical literalist, Barth insisted that there are only two approaches to knowing God. He said one begins

# 3 ONE PEOPLE: IN THE PROPHETS

with humans and one begins with God – and only the latter is reliable.

John Macquarrie is one who has taken the former approach, insisting that God conforms to what human reason says he should be like. This caused him to dismiss one particular doctrine because it offended his human sensibilities.

"This is a doctrine which, even if it could claim support from the Bible or the history of theology, would still have to be rejected because of the affront which it offers to reason and conscience."[78]

Macquarrie also said.

"We see Christology as a kind of transcendent anthropology."[79]

Barth challenged this approach with indignation.

"One cannot speak of God simply by speaking of man in a loud voice."[80] "God is in heaven, and thou art on earth."[81]

**Trying to fashion God according to our subjective wish lists is a dangerous business, and one doomed to failure.** One writer describes the futility of any attempt.

"[Subjectivism] is like a sheep overwhelmed in the snowdrift trying to keep itself alive by feeding on its own ideas." – T.F. Torrance[82]

**We need to take to heart the warnings about making our own 'golden calf-gods' in the formation of a God we can 'cope with', or even manage or fully understand.**

"Nothing which is true or beautiful or good makes complete sense in any immediate context of history; therefore we must be saved by faith." – Reinhold Niebuhr[83]

"I cannot completely believe in a God that I can understand completely." – Loralee Hagan[84]

A golden calf is unworthy of worship, unable to help anyone, and exists only because of the 'creative' imagina-

> **He looked like glowing metal, as if full of fire, … and brilliant light surrounded him.**

tion of its makers; so too the false 'godettes' we might be tempted to construct. God is the awesome Holy One. He is the One who commanded Moses to take off his shoes, because footwear has to go when we're standing on holy ground; he is the object of sacrificial worship of the Tabernacle and Temple. He is the Holy One that Isaiah encountered in the Temple, prompting the prophet to cry out in awe and coin his favourite term: 'The Holy One of Israel' (Isa 1:4, 5:19, 10:20). Yet, as we will see, he is also the God of Hosea, the Holy One in our midst (Hos 11:6). Holiness is, in Old Testament thinking, the very inwardness of God's being. It is his nature, his 'Godness.'

## The great stranger – yet God is not watching us 'from a distance'

"O Lord God Almighty, who is like you? You are mighty, O Lord, and your faithfulness surrounds you." – Psalm 89:8

The word 'holy' means 'marked off from the ordinary' – God cannot be rationalised or dumbed down. Some writers have called this quality of holiness 'the great stranger', because it is unique. God's purity is perfect, his power is beyond understanding, he is 'the beautiful One' (Psa 27:4). The holiness of God means that in no sense is God 'one of us'.

"The holy could more aptly be designated the great stranger in the human world, that is, a datum of experience which can never really be coordinated into the world in which humans are at home, and over against which he initially feels fear rather than trust – it is in fact, the 'wholly other.'"     – *Gerhard von Rad*[85]

Rudolph Otto's book *The Idea of the Holy* focuses on the *mysterium tremendum*, the sense of awe that human beings feel when in the presence of vast transcendence. Perhaps the American writer Annie Dillard was influenced by Otto's thinking when she rightly cautioned us against trivialising God.

"The churches are children playing on the floor with their chemistry sets, mixing up a batch to kill on a Sunday morning. It is madness to wear ladies straw hats and velvet hats to church; we should all be wearing crash helmets. Ushers should issue life preservers and signal flares; they should lash us to our pews. For the sleeping God may wake some day and take offence; the waking God may draw us out to where we can never return."     – *Annie Dillard*[86]

The biblical call to come near to the throne of God with confidence (Heb 10:22) means that Dillard surely overstates her case. But perhaps we should remind ourselves of just how remarkable that invitation is; under the old covenant, even Isaiah could only cower until his lips have been cleansed with a burning coal (Isa 6:6). The human response to this 'awful' holiness must be an overwhelming feeling of unworthiness and insignificance. In Isaiah this sense is expressed most strongly in the refrain of a poem.

"Go into the rocks, hide in the ground from dread of the LORD and the splendour of his majesty!"     – *Isaiah 2:10*

The echoes of Isaiah's vision of God seated on the throne in the Temple are heard again in the great opening vision of Ezekiel, the Chariot-Throne of God with the four living creatures.

"I saw that from what appeared to be his waist up he looked like glowing metal, as if full of fire, and that from there down he looked like fire; and brilliant light surrounded him. Like the appearance of a rainbow in the clouds on a rainy day, so was the radiance around him. This was the appearance of the likeness of the glory of the LORD. When I saw it, I fell face down, and I heard the voice of one speaking."     – *Ezekiel 1:27–28*

This echo of Isaiah 6 in its turn is echoed by the climax of Daniel's vision of the night, where he saw the Ancient of Days on a throne 'flaming with fire' (Dan 7:9) being approached by 'one like a son of man'.

A reminder of the awesomeness of God is timely, lest we replace our confidence with a casual 'God is my mate' approach: a God who deserves no reverence surely has no relevance.

"Reverence and awe have often been replaced by a yawn of familiarity. The consuming fire has been domesticated into a candle flame, adding a bit of religious atmosphere, perhaps, but no heat, no blinding light, no power for purification."     – *Donald McCullough*[87]

The story of God does not stop with the revelation of his holy transcendence. Israel's story is that a 'wholly other' God has *connected* with them, defining their religion and shaping their ethics. This is a distinctive God who unites himself with people. Ultimately their union is dynamically fulfilled in the incarnation of Christ, as this *wholly other* God becomes God *wholly for us*; Emmanuel, God with us. God's holiness is expressed both by his *immanence* – the One who is with us – and his *transcendence* – the One who is high above all. Yet the Holy One in the midst of his people (Hos 11:9) is a portrait which emerges from the earliest chapters of Genesis.

"The God of the prophets is not the wholly other, a strange, weird, uncanny Being, shrouded in unfathomable darkness, but the God of the covenant, whose will they know and are called upon to convey. The God they proclaim is not the Remote One, but the One who is invoked, near, and concerned." – *Rabbi Abraham Heschel*[88]

Far from being unapproachable, or the one watching us from a distance, he comes looking for us and comes to save. The holiness cultic provisions of the Old Testament make approaching God possible; the terms of the approach were set by him to allow unholy humans proximity to the Holy God (Exod 19:12, 21, 24).

"Then the man and his wife heard the sound of the Lord God as he was walking in the garden in the cool of the day, and they hid from the Lord God among the trees of the garden. But the Lord God called to the man, 'Where are you?'"
– *Genesis 3:8*

**God the Holy One is involved; and he is the God who is love.** He calls his people 'my treasured possession' (his *segullah* or treasure, Exod 19:5), and loves them with a familial, protective and caring love, like the love of a father, a mother or a spouse, prepared to go to any lengths, as we see in Hosea 2:19 (the passionate love of the spouse – 'I will betroth you to me for ever') and Hosea 11:4 (the tender, caring love of the parent – 'I led them with cords of human kindness, with ties of love').

God's love is also expressed in his forgiving nature. He continued to sustain his Old Testament people, forgiving their idolatry and turning from judgement (Exod 32). The provision of forgiveness for human failure is one of the salient features of the religion of Israel. The logical Greeks could not rise to forgiveness; their gods presided only over vengeance. The endless cycle of revenge continues relentlessly through *The Oresteia* as well as *The Oedipus Trilogy*. The heart of Greek tragedy is that fate is inevitable and cannot be turned aside. Mercy plays no role there. By contrast, standing as a banner headline over Israel's concept of God is the revelation of his gracious compassionate nature.

"The LORD, the LORD, the compassionate and gracious God, slow to anger, abounding in love and faithfulness, maintaining love to thousands, and forgiving wickedness, rebellion and sin."
– *Exodus 34:6–7*

**Yahweh revealed his name to Moses at the Burning Bush, but gives its meaning only when the first massive failure of the covenant has occurred.** It is then that God's tender character is fully revealed. This passage is alluded to again and again throughout the scriptures, in the ancient promise to David (Psa 89:16) that God's faithful love and forgiveness will never desert his descendants, in Jeremiah's purchase of a field as a guarantee of return from captivity (Jer 32:18), and in Jonah's satirical petulance when his threats of disaster on Nineveh are foiled by their appeal to God's forgiveness.

"O LORD, is this not what I said when I was still at home? That is why I was so quick to flee to Tarshish. I knew that you are a gracious and compassionate God, slow to anger and abounding in love, a God who relents from sending calamity."
– *Jonah 4:2*

**And this slow to anger God is also so incredibly patient with a stubborn people.**

"A human being is holy not because he or she triumphs by will power over chaos and guilt and leads a flawless life, but because that life shows the victory of God's faithfulness in the midst of disorder and imperfection. The church is holy… not because it is the gathering of the good and the well behaved, but because it speaks of the triumph of grace in the coming together of strangers and sinners, who, miraculously trust one another enough to join in common repentance and common praise. … Humanly speaking, holiness is always like this: God's endurance in the middle of our refusal of him, his capacity to meet every refusal with the gift of himself."
– *Rowan Williams*[89]

God the Holy One loves. But 'love' is a word that has been cheapened; this holy love is far more than sentimentality.

## God the Holy One: love beyond kindness

"Love is central in God, but holiness is central in love."
— *Augustus H. Strong*[90]

"And you have forgotten the exhortation that addresses you as children—'My child, do not regard lightly the discipline of the Lord, or lose heart when you are punished by him; for the Lord disciplines those whom he loves, and chastises every child whom he accepts.' Endure trials for the sake of discipline. God is treating you as children; for what child is there whom a parent does not discipline? If you do not have that discipline in which all children share, then you are illegitimate and not his children. Moreover, we had human parents to discipline us, and we respected them. Should we not be even more willing to be subject to the Father of spirits and live? For they disciplined us for a short time as seemed best to them, but he disciplines us for our good, in order that we may share his holiness."
— *Hebrews 12:5–10* (NRSV)

Sometimes the *holiness* of God seems to be set as an antithesis to the truth about the love of God. There is a danger that we can sentimentalise God, and develop romantic notions rather than embrace biblical truths about his being. There is no contradiction between the two truths; indeed, God disciplines *because* he loves (Heb 12:6). Any parent who has ever told a child 'This is good for you,' and then administered punishment, cough medicine or anything other than what the child would actually prefer, knows that love transcends kindness.

"Kindness… cares not whether its object becomes good or bad, provided only that it escapes suffering. As scripture points out, it is bastards who are spoiled: the legitimate sons, who are to carry on the family tradition, are punished. It is for people who we care nothing about that we demand happiness on any terms: with our friends, our lovers, our children, we are exacting and would rather see them suffer much than be happy in contemptible and estranging modes. If God is Love, he is, by definition, something more than

mere kindness. And it appears, from all records, that though he has often rebuked and condemned us, he has never regarded us with contempt. He has paid us the intolerable compliment of loving us, in the deepest, most tragic, most inexorable sense."
— *C.S. Lewis*[91]

"We should speak less of the love of God and more of his holiness – so that when we did speak of his love we would have something more to say."
— *P.T. Forsyth*

"Love in action is a harsh and dreadful thing compared with love in dreams."
— *Father Zossima in Fyodor Dostoevsky's* The Brothers Karamazov

> **Holiness is never a ladder that humanity climbs to reach God, but the response of love to love.**

T.S. Eliot sums up this truth of the blazing fire of love that is holiness, and he described love as 'the unfamiliar name' of even God's judgement, in *Little Gidding* (No. 4 of 'Four Quartets').

The dove descending breaks the air
With flame of incandescent terror
Of which the tongues declare
The one discharge from sin and error.
The only hope, or else despair
Lies in the choice of pyre or pyre –
To be redeemed from fire by fire.

Who then devised the torment? Love.
Love is the unfamiliar Name
Behind the hands that wove
The intolerable shirt of flame
Which human power cannot remove

# 3 ONE PEOPLE: IN THE PROPHETS

We only live, only suspire
Consumed by either fire or fire.

## God the Holy One: initiation, imitation and the family likeness

Holiness is a **response** to the person and activity of God. The Old Testament reveals him as the one who intervened with grace and redeeming action, who then calls his people to respond to his initiative; an interventionist God, directing the course of history.

"Holiness was the defining characteristic and desired purpose for Israel, God's covenant people. It was the attribute by which the people of God were to be distinguished from all the other nations. This is explicitly stated by God when he constitutes the nation of Israel at Mount Sinai as his chosen covenant people."
– *Richard Longenecker*[92]

"God's 'holiness' is rooted in the fact that God is 'the wholly other', different from all other beings. So, God's people are called to be 'holy' by living differently from other people. Keeping the law was not just an arbitrary 'response' to God, but an appropriate one, since it enabled Israel to express something of the 'otherness' of God by living differently from the people around them. It was meant to be a difference that attracted, not repelled, people (Matt 5:16)."
– *Ernest Lucas*[93]

**Holiness is therefore never a ladder that humanity climbs in order to reach God, or an impersonal set of ethics, but the response of love to love.** This reciprocal pattern is a thread that runs throughout the Bible's moral teaching. Jesus calls us to love each other as *he has loved us* (John 15:12). Our fellowship is a response to his proactive love.

"We love because he first loved us."
– *1 John 4:19*

"Some people think that the Old Testament, in contrast to the New, taught that redemption was achieved by keeping the law. But it does not. There too, God's grace comes first, and man's response second."
– *Chris Wright*[94]

**And because holiness is 'the biblical shorthand'[95] for the very essence of God, so God's people are called to be like him, to walk in his ways.**

"Speak to the entire assembly of Israel and say to them: 'Be holy because I, the Lord your God, am holy.'"
– *Leviticus 19:2*

This call to imitation is extended into New Testament thinking.

"Be perfect, therefore, as your heavenly Father is perfect."
– *Matthew 5:48*

"Be imitators of God, therefore, as dearly loved children and live a life of love, just as Christ loved us and gave himself up for us as a fragrant offering and sacrifice to God."
– *Ephesians 5:1–2*

**Knowing the Holy God and becoming like him will therefore always sit at the heart of true holiness; morality and intimacy married together.**

**One Holy, Catholic, Apostolic People**

## So what? Person to Person: For individual reflection

- *THE HORSE AND His Boy* by C.S. Lewis is the story of Shasta and the talking horse Bree, who are joined by the escaping pair of Aravis and Hwin. When Aravis describes Aslan, the great deliverer of Narnia, Bree scoffs at her idea that Aslan might actually be a real lion. In his mocking, he doesn't notice that Aravis and her horse Hwin are staring wide-eyed at something on the wall behind him.

"While Bree spoke they saw an enormous lion leap up from outside and balance itself on top of the green wall; only it was a brighter yellow and it was bigger and more beautiful and more alarming than any lion they had ever seen. And at once it jumped down inside the wall and began approaching Bree from behind. It made no noise at all. And Hwin and Aravis couldn't make any noise themselves, no more than if they were frozen.

'No doubt,' continued Bree, 'when they speak of him as a Lion they only mean he is as strong as a lion or (to our enemies, of course) as fierce as a lion. Or something of that kind. Even a little girl like you, Aravis, must see it would be quite absurd to suppose he is a real lion. Indeed it would be disrespectful. If he was a lion he would have to be a Beast just like the rest of us. Why!' (and here Bree began to laugh)

'If he was a lion he would have four paws, and a tail and *Whiskers*! … Aie, ooh, hoo-hoo! Help!'

For just as he said the word *Whiskers* one of Aslan's had actually tickled his ear. Bree shot away like an arrow to the other side of the enclosure and there turned; the wall was too high for him to jump and he could fly no farther. Aravis and Hwin both started back. …

'Now, Bree,' he said, 'you poor, proud, frightened Horse, draw near. Nearer still, my son. Do not dare not to dare. Touch me. Smell me. Here are my paws, here is my tail, these are my whiskers. I am a true Beast.'

'Aslan,' said Bree in a shaken voice, 'I'm afraid I must be rather a fool.'

'Happy the Horse who knows that while he is still young. Or the Human either.'[96]

Ask yourself, **How am I when I encounter elements of faith that stretch my understanding? Have I become more certain since I came to faith, or am I more at home with mystery? What aspects of God cause me struggle? Is there freedom in my being able to confess that 'I am a fool'?**

# 3 ONE PEOPLE: IN THE PROPHETS

## So what? Small Groups: For discussion together

### Demolishing our god factories

As Donald McCullough points out in his challenging and wonderful book *The Trivialization of God: The Dangerous Illusion of a Manageable Deity*, the gods we manufacture for ourselves can include:

- THE GOD OF **My Cause** – we begin with an idea or a conviction, and then make scripture, and therefore God, endorse our thinking.
- THE GOD OF **My Understanding** – rushing to draw huge distinctions between our views (orthodoxy) and those with whom we disagree (those in error), and where arrogance makes us bomb others with 'jihads of theological self-assuredness'.[97]
- THE GOD OF **My Experience** – where we define spirituality for *all* by the spiritual experiences of *our* journey, and insist that other experiences of God mirror ours.

The three gods above can be a problem for all of us, whatever our theological background, but McCullough wisely points out that liberals might be more vulnerable to the god of political correctness, conservative evangelicals more tempted by the god of theological correctness, and charismatics more prone to the worship of the god of experiential correctness.[98]

- THE GOD OF **My Comfort** – here God is the mechanism I rely upon to satisfy me and make me happy (health and wealth prosperity teaching would be an example), and where love is seen as the antithesis of judgement or discipline.
- THE GOD OF **My Success** – we define success superficially, and forget that Jesus, poor, powerless and despised on a Roman cross, is the ultimate 'success' story.
- THE GOD OF **My Nation** – where loyalty, national identity and discipleship become tangled and confused, and the assumption is made that God is 'on our side' while we fail to ask if we are on his side.

**What 'golden calf' gods do you think we in the British church are most likely to make?**

**Given that we live in a world where 'signs of otherness' and transcendence are being eradicated from public consciousness, do we teach and preach a version of the Christian God that we've picked off a shelf to meet our own consumerist needs?**

**Are we down the mountain busily making golden calves like there's no tomorrow, but there's no mountain top to be seen, let alone any cloud, mountain or tablets of stone?**

# Distinctive People: Holiness Snapshots

The U2 song 'Yahweh' expresses a desperate longing for the unclean to be made pure, and for the heart and 'stranded' soul to be renewed and reconnected to the Holy God:

> **Take this shirt**
> **Polyester white trash made in nowhere**
> **Take this shirt**
> **And make it clean, clean**
> **Take this soul**
> **Stranded in some skin and bones**
>
> *– U2 'Yahweh'*99

But we must go beyond heartfelt aspiration and understand what it actually means for us to be a holy people. God revealed himself in the Old Testament as the Holy One, and called his people to become like him – but then gave a clear picture of what the holy life should look like. Old Testament holiness **teaching** came to full flower in the prophets and histories.

Despite this, **the story of the Old Testament people of God, from their beginnings but especially during the period of the prophets and histories, is one of rebellion and a complete misunderstanding of the true nature of holiness.**

The holiness that God was looking for included faithfulness from his people as well as worship that transcended empty piety and had a social conscience.

- ELIJAH, IN THE Mount Carmel showdown, stands as the outstanding example of confronting Israel with the truth that **holiness means loyalty** and the rejection of all other gods (1 Kings 18:20–46).
- SAMUEL THE PROPHET called the people to have no other king but the Lord (1 Sam 8:10–18).
- ISAIAH, AMOS AND Micah showed Israel the **utter futility of pious ceremony and 'worship' that was meaningless, and indeed offensive to God, if they continued to oppress the poor and weak** (Isa 1:13–17, cf. Isa 58, Micah 3), with Amos warning of exile to come (Amos 5:2,27), a common theme of all of the eighth-century prophets.

**And the prophets caught a glimpse of the fullness of holiness that was to come in the Messiah.**

- ISAIAH POINTED THE way to **the age of the Spirit** (6:1–8; 32:15,17; 35:8–10; 44:3; 59:19,21; 62:12, with the solemn warning of 63:7–10).
- JEREMIAH WROTE OF the '**new covenant**' (31:31–33; cf. Heb 10:14–22).
- EZEKIEL'S PROMISE OF the cleansing **to come from the 'new spirit'** within (36:25–26,29).
- JOEL FAMOUSLY PREDICTED the **Day of Pentecost outpouring** (2:28–29).
- ZECHARIAH HAD A vision of the '**fountain … opened for sin and for uncleanness**' (12:10; 13:1,9).
- MALACHI PROPHESIED THE Messiah's **refining fire that would purify** and purge and make possible 'an offering in righteousness' (3:1–3).

But the *lifestyles* of the people of God at that time were sadly lacking. In short, Israel traded holiness for survival and lost sight of their purpose and priority as a 'sanctified' people; they traded distinctiveness for syncretism, and swapped transformation for a cycle of endless rebellion, and purity for debauchery.

## Sanctified: the purpose driven life

"They will be called the Holy People, the Redeemed of the Lord; and you will be called Sought After, the City No Longer Deserted."

*– Isaiah 62:12*

"Therefore, I urge you, brothers, in view of God's mercy, to offer your bodies as living sacrifices, holy and pleasing to God—this is your spiritual act of worship."

*– Romans 12:1*

The Hebrew word for 'holy' that Moses used in Leviticus means 'that which is set apart and marked off, that which is different.' The Sabbath was holy because God set it apart for his people (Exod 16:23). The priests were holy because they were set apart to minister to the Lord (Lev 21:7–8). Their garments were holy and could not be used for common use (Exod 28:2). The tithe that the people brought was holy (Lev 27:30). Anything that God declared holy was to be treated differently from the common things of life in the Hebrew camp. In fact, the camp of Israel itself was holy, because the Lord dwelt there with his people (Deut 23:14).

The related word 'sanctify' comes from the Latin *sanctus*, which means 'consecrated, sacred, blameless.'

But Israel fell into a cyclical pattern of rebellion, repentance, restitution and then rebellion again. The covenant with Yahweh would be renewed, often with tears (Jdg 2:4–5), but before long the rot would set in yet again. The lament in the early part of Judges paints a drab, seemingly hopeless picture.

"After Joshua had dismissed the Israelites, they went to take possession of the land, each to his own inheritance. The people served the LORD throughout the lifetime of Joshua and of the elders who outlived him and who had seen all the great things the LORD had done for Israel. Joshua son of Nun, the servant of the LORD, died at the age of a hundred and ten. And they buried him in the land of his inheritance, at Timnath Heres in the hill country of Ephraim, north of Mount Gaash. After that whole generation had been gathered to their fathers, another generation grew up, who knew neither the LORD nor what he had done for Israel. Then the Israelites did evil in the eyes of the LORD and served the Baals. They forsook the LORD, the God of their fathers, who had brought them out of Egypt. They followed and worshipped various gods of the peoples around them. They provoked the LORD to anger because they forsook him and served Baal and the Ashtoreths. In his anger against Israel the LORD handed them over to raiders who plundered them. He sold them to their enemies all around, whom they were no longer able to resist. Whenever Israel went out to fight, the hand of the LORD was against them to defeat them, just as he had sworn to them. They were in great distress. Then the LORD raised up judges, who saved them out of the hands of these raiders. Yet they would not listen to their judges but prostituted themselves to other gods and worshipped them. Unlike their fathers, they quickly turned from the way in which their fathers had walked, the way of obedience to the Lord's commands. Whenever the LORD raised up a judge for them, he was with the judge and saved them out of the hands of their enemies as long as the judge lived; for the LORD had compassion on them as they groaned under those who oppressed and afflicted them. But when the judge died, the people returned to ways even more corrupt than those of their fathers, following other gods and serving and worshipping them. They refused to give up their evil practices and stubborn ways."

*– Judges 2:6–19*

It was to their loss: sin stole so many opportunities for Israel to enjoy the dynamic purpose for which they had been created as a people.

One **Holy**, Catholic, Apostolic People

The word 'holy' has taken on a musty image, implying that the holy are those who are steeped in lifeless and empty traditionalism, who are struggling to maintain the status quo in a rapidly changing world. Sainthood evokes images of ethereal dreamers somewhat disconnected from the real world, so overwhelmingly irrelevant is their piety. But holiness is really a dynamic attitude of wholehearted availability to the purposes of our dynamic God. Responding to change and being flexible becomes the natural stance for the genuinely holy, because the priority question is always 'What is God asking of us as his instruments of purpose?' rather than whining about our own preferences and potential discomforts.

> Shalom – the peace with God that leads to peace within ourselves, peace with each other.

Sometimes the concept of being sanctified – set apart, or separated – has been overlaid with negative notions of retreat into the safety of cloisters, because we are fearful and nervous about living in the real world where we are called to deal with all the assaults and power of sin. But again, this separation is dynamic and positive. The great news is that God has decided to partner with humanity in his ongoing agenda for the universe; the responsive choice that we have is to live, as the worship song affirms, 'for something that will last forever'.

> "In particular, holiness is a positive attribute or status, not a negative one…. It is as much separated for as separated from."
> – *Philip Jensen*[100]

But the people of purpose *will* be different and distinctive.

## Different: syncretism and shalom

> "Do not conform any longer to the pattern of this world." – Romans 12:2a

> "When you enter the land the Lord your God is giving you, do not learn to imitate the detestable ways of the nations there."
> – *Deuteronomy 18:9*

> "Now appoint a king to lead us, such as all the other nations have."
> – *1 Samuel 8:5b*

Holiness is an event that leads to a changed life: we are made holy, and we are becoming holy. Holiness is not non-conformity in the development of a superficially alternative lifestyle, where the people of God 'stand out' because they are odd, but where they choose to mirror the character of God and walk in his ways. His is the drumbeat to which they march. But Israel longed to get in step with other tired old tunes, and consistently failed to appreciate her unique relationship with God as the only King she would ever need.

Canaanite religion was similar in some respects to the religion of Israel.

- Offerings of sheep and cattle were given in worship.
- A priesthood existed, with a high priest taking charge of twelve priestly families.
- The Canaanites had priestly scribes to care for their sacred writings. Like Israel, their festivals were based around the farming year, as one would expect of an agrarian culture.
- They had psalmists who would sing liturgies in their ceremonies.
- There were prophets who would speak on behalf of their gods.
- They even had a god of covenant, Baal Berith – the lord of the covenant – who was worshipped at Shechem.

The problem of similarity was further compounded by the fact that the Canaanite Baal cult revered a bull as an animal sacred to Baal. Culturally, the idea of a bull as an object of worship was very strong. Thus Israel became easily drawn into bull worship, most obviously as they worshipped the

# 3 ONE PEOPLE: IN THE PROPHETS

## Humanifesto

I want to be a grace guerrilla,
No longer a chameleon of karma:
The time has come to stand out
From the crowd.
I want to give forgiveness
A fighting chance
Of freeing me,
To live in love,
And live it out loud

I want to drink deep
Of the foolishness of wisdom,
Instead of swallowing
The wisdom of fools:
To find a source
In the deeper mines of meaning.
I want to search-out the unsearchable
To invoke the invisible:
To choose the truths
The TV hypnotists aren't screening.

No camouflage
No entourage
No smoothly fitting-in
I want a faith that goes further than face-value
And a beauty that goes deeper than my skin.

I want to be untouched by my possessions,
Instead of being possessed
By what I touch:
To test the taste
Of having nothing to call mine:
To hold consumption's cravings back;
To be content with luck or lack
To live as well on water as on wine.

I want to spend myself
On those I think might need me,
Not spend
All I think I need on myself:
I want my heart
To be willing to make house-calls.
Let those whose rope is at an end
Find in me a faithful friend,
Let me be known as one who re-builds broken walls.

No camouflage
No entourage
No smoothly fitting-in
I want a faith that goes further than face-value
And a beauty that goes deeper than my skin.

I want to be centred outside the circle
To be chiselled from a different seam
I want to be seduced by another story
And drawn into a deeper dream
To be anchored in an undiscovered ocean,
To revolve around an unfamiliar sun;
A boom-box tuned to an alternate station;
A bullet fired from a different gun.

No camouflage
No entourage
No smoothly fitting-in
I want a faith that goes further than face-value
And a beauty that goes deeper than my skin.

– Gerard Kelly[101]

One **Holy**, Catholic, Apostolic People

golden calf in the Sinai wilderness (Exod 32). Hosea would lament with sarcasm that they 'kiss the calf-idols' (Hos 13:2) although people would not have thought of themselves as worshipping the calves, but the god whom they represented. Baal was described as the Rider of the Clouds, who sits on a heavenly throne and hurls down thunderbolts, and Yahweh is described in exactly the same terms (Psa 2:4; 18:13; 77:18; 103:19; 144:6).

**Israel's affections were harnessed by the subtle wooing that comes when you are surrounded by a so-called 'similar' religion: 'This isn't so different from our way, is it?' Seduced by what seem similar, Israel consistently rebelled against God.**

Not only did this rebellion have huge social consequences, with the oppressive practices of royal households aping the absolute monarchical systems of other nations from the reign of Solomon onwards, but Israel's waywardness was also a total rejection of God as her sole Lord. This syncretism – becoming the same as other nations and mingling their cultures with Israel's to produce a hybrid – was a serious matter, tantamount to spiritual adultery against the Lord, who demanded their sole allegiance (Jer 3; Ezek 16; Hos 2). **In times of ease, Israel allowed herself to be carried along by influential immigrants like the wife of a king; pressure, exile and external military threat, ironically, helped her to remember who she was.**

**God called his people to a theocratic radicalism that would permeate her whole existence. Israel was invited to be an alternative society, and not just because of her style of worship, modes of dress or diet. Her radicalism was to be expressed politically, in her choice of God over a human king; socially, in her care for the poor and the marginalized; economically and environmentally, in the way she saw the land as God's gift and not her right, and was steward of it; theologically, because she had encountered the self-revelation of God and would not dabble in the god-constructing habits of her idolatrous neighbours. Israel was never called to 'fit in'. And neither are we.**

**One word summarizes this radical whole of life holiness – shalom. Shalom speaks of the peace with God that leads to peace within ourselves, peace with each other, peace with our environment, and peace between groups and nations. Shalom means much more than cessation of war. It includes blessings such as wholeness, health, quietness of soul, preservation and completeness. The reality of the kingdom of God, which we will consider carefully tomorrow, demonstrates the corporate nature of holiness.**

" [Shalom] is related to the whole of life and to the whole world, to the individual, the family, society, the social and personal. It is immediate and it is ultimate. It is universal and inclusive. It is historical, eschatological and eternal. It is a daily experience, a constant possibility, a final hope. Nothing, no-one, is beyond the range of this word."
– *Jim Punton*[102]

" The Old Testament …[uses] one treasure-chest word, shalom. Shalom, translated 'peace,' proves when unpacked to mean, not just freedom from war and trouble, sin and irreligion, but also justice, prosperity, good fellowship, and health, and all-round communal well-being under God's gracious hand." – *Jim Packer*

Shalom is the rounded peace that is rooted in God: 'What is your peace?' is the way Jews often greet one another; and the response is, 'My peace is from the Lord, for I trust wholly in him.'

The Irish theologian, Enda McDonagh, defines shalom as 'a rich reality of wholeness; a sense of well-being and flourishing' of the human spirit that involves the human being feeling connected to God by being in balance with all of creation. Shalom is both a *gift* and a *task*. The primary characteristics of shalom are peace and justice. In the Hebrew, the peace of shalom is a harmony of body, mind, spirit and emotion – a sense of balance, wholeness and well being. The Hebrew word for justice is *sedaqah*, meaning 'righteousness' – to live in right relationship with all of creation. According to McDonagh, in the Hebrew tradition

# 3 ONE PEOPLE: IN THE PROPHETS

this requires faithfulness, mercy, kindness and love. In this view, we can't really live in justice if we don't have all of these features in our lives. McDonagh points out that through the ages, successive translations of the Christian scriptures have narrowed and distorted our understanding of peace and justice – of shalom. In Greek versions of scripture there are more that twenty terms used to try to describe the concept of shalom. The nearest Greek word is *eirene*, which means harmony and order and therefore lacks the sense of right relationship with the Creator and his creation contained within shalom. When the scriptures are translated into Latin, the nearest word for shalom is *pax*, meaning legal order, which is a long way from shalom with its wholeness, well-being and flourishing of the spirit in balance with creation. Similarly, translations of *sedaqah* end up with the Latin word *justitia*, in English justice. But this Western concept has stressed the rights of the individual and their entitlements, with much less focus on the gift and task of living in right relationships.[103] (From an address by Brendan McAllister, Director of Mediation Northern Ireland.)

As Israelite society shifted from its agricultural roots to a more urban and commercial society, the prophets increasingly cried out against wrong relationships that were corrupted by the twin viruses of greed and injustice. God's law envisioned a peaceful society in which each person rested safely under his own vine and fig tree (1 Kings 4:25; Micah 4:4). Yet when Israel became prosperous, as in the days of Jeroboam II, a wealthy upper class developed. The old values embedded in the law of mutual aid and sharing were replaced by selfishness and indifference to the poor. Thus Amos, in Jeroboam's day, cried out against oppression of the poor by the rich (Amos 2:6–7), against indifference toward the hungry (6:3–6), and against corruption in the courts (2:7; 8:6) as well as against immorality (2:7).

In these days, when the church is constantly being called to relevance, we should beware the danger of defining our distinctiveness superficially, where we congratulate ourselves that we stand out because we adhere to the basic norms of a Christian subculture and yet fail to live differently in the deeper issues.

A Christian denomination, in a bid to recover a holiness culture, recently reiterated its absolute prohibition on the use of alcohol or nicotine. The use of alcohol is generally more acceptable among UK Christians than it was thirty years ago, so we surely need clearer teaching and account-ability about alcohol abuse and alcoholism, but there are other issues in which our distinctiveness must also be demonstrated.

That same denomination has made no appraisal of the ethics of the war in Iraq, sometimes it uses leadership practices that abuse power, and it largely dismisses concern about the environment 'because it's all going to be destroyed in the end times anyway'. Holiness can thus be reduced to the ticking of a few markers that are for the most part culturally generated, and by which it is assumed that we are either 'in' or 'out'.

If the depth that is *shalom* is to be a reality, it will have to come as a result of our being transformed by God's Spirit daily at work in our lives.

## Transformation: becoming what we are

"Consecrate yourselves and be holy, because I am the LORD your God. Keep my decrees and follow them. I am the LORD, who makes you holy." – *Leviticus 20:7–8*

"… be transformed by the renewing of your mind. Then you will be able to test and approve what God's will is." – *Romans 12:2*

Both God and humans are involved in the decision to sanctify and then in the ongoing process of sanctifica-tion. In both Old and New Testament thinking, the decision to set something, or someone, apart as holy begins with God, is rooted in his initiative, and yet, as we shall see momentarily, is further made real in the response of humanity. In the Old Testament, God's people were exposed to the power of transformation by being exposed

One **Holy**, Catholic, Apostolic People

to the truth of his word, by participating in the experience of the *cultus* (the religious ceremonies and festivals), and also by the chastening discipline of judgement. God's holiness brings judgement upon sin, but the purpose of that judgement is not destructive but redemptive.

- WHEN GOD ACTS to save, it is to vindicate his holiness before all people (Ezek 36:22–32).
- As WE'VE NOTED, when Isaiah preaches forgiveness and redemption, he calls the God of mercy the Holy One of Israel (Isa 10:20; 12:6; 29:19).
- HOSEA IN PARTICULAR demonstrates how holiness is expressed in conquering holy love, which is rooted in the covenantal bond of grace.

## Sin is the catastrophe that robs and rapes, and steals our humanity.

And so the people of God were, and are, not left alone and commanded to struggle to become what they were not; even in judging his people, God is actively involved with them. They were called holy, and called to become holy.

"The sacred is not, but has to be brought into being as the result of someone's action or behaviour. Israel is made holy by God, and becomes holy by sanctifying itself."
— *Rabbi Eliezer Berkovits*[104]

"It requires a special act of God to make a thing or person holy."[105]

The same is true of us today. There are three aspects of sanctification: positional, practical, and perfect. The process

of holiness is rooted in what God has done, what God is doing, and what God will do.

- **POSITIONAL SANCTIFICATION** MEANS that the believer is once-and-for-all set apart for God (1 Cor 1:2; 6:9–11; Heb 10:10).
- **PRACTICAL SANCTIFICATION** IS the process by which the believer daily becomes more like Christ (John 17:17; 2 Cor 3:18; 7:1).
- **PERFECT SANCTIFICATION** IS our experience when we see Christ in fullness (1 John 3:2). We are saved, and made holy, to become holy in Christ (Eph 1:4; 5:27; Col 1:22). Holiness is not about woodenly fulfilling a set of principles; it is being changed in the unfolding drama of daily friendship with God and God's people.

And this distinctive, transformed life of holiness is wonderful.

### Purity: catastrophe and euchatastrophe

"… his good, pleasing and perfect will." – *Romans 12:2b*

"The glory of God is a human who is alive." – *Irenaeus*

Holiness leads to shalom, which, far from being a weird, unnatural life where we deny ourselves what every 'normal' person should enjoy, is actually the discovery of what it means to be wonderfully alive, to discover authentic joy. A negative view of holiness is perpetuated by a church that too often is suspicious of laughter, is in denial about the power and pleasure of sexuality, and mistakes intensity for passion. But it is *sin* that is truly gloomy – not the life of faith.

The pattern of rebellion ultimately led God's people into exile: the place of sadness, shame and utter loss of hope.

"By the rivers of Babylon we sat and wept when we remembered Zion. There on the poplars we hung our harps, for there our captors asked us for songs, our tormentors demanded songs of joy; they said, 'Sing us one of the songs of Zion!'"
— *Psalm 137:1–3*

Beyond the actual experience of exile, sin is revealed as the muddy pool rather than the well of pure water. The prophets constantly warned the people away from 'the bread that does not satisfy', and promised not only nourishment and feasting but delight and true life – and, through them, life to the nations if they would only return to God. Consider Isaiah's' call.

"Come, all you who are thirsty, come to the waters; and you who have no money, come, buy and eat! Come, buy wine and milk without money and without cost. Why spend money on what is not bread, and your labour on what does not satisfy? Listen, listen to me, and eat what is good, and your soul will delight in the richest of fare. Give ear and come to me; hear me, that your soul may live. I will make an everlasting covenant with you, my faithful love promised to David. See, I have made him a witness to the peoples, a leader and commander of the peoples. Surely you will summon nations you know not, and nations that do not know you will hasten to you, because of the LORD your God, the Holy One of Israel, for he has endowed you with splendour."
– *Isaiah 55:1–5*

Sin is the catastrophe that robs and rapes, and steals our humanity. It's an extreme example, but one that is worthy of our consideration. The Nazis knew this when they designed the death camps of the holocaust. Not content to ferry millions to the ovens, they sought to kill Jews even while they lived by consistently profaning the holy, in a strategy so repulsive that one writer describes it as 'excremental assault'.[106] In the death camps, 'whatever a human being ever cherished was degraded'.[107] Auschwitz had no sanitary facilities, except one tap that Jewish women were forbidden to use.[108]

"The absence of sanitary facilities in the women's camp of 14,000 women was… a deliberate way of erasing the humanity of women, condemning them to die in and as excrement. The surface of the body was broken and covered over by lice and fleas, encrusted with mud and

filth, suppurating sores and boils, cracked by sunburn and frostbite."
– *Melissa Raphael*[109]

This dehumanising strategy meant that a prisoner was never addressed by name, but referred to as a number; her stench and appearance further prohibited approach, touch, relationship and the possibility of being known.[110] Jewishness itself was specifically fouled, with a programme of routine desecration of the holy. Some women were forced to wear torn-up pieces of *talles* (prayer shawls) as underclothes. Others were given strips of prayer shawls to keep their ill fitting shoes on.

"By this means, the symbols and possibilities of prayer were trodden into the mud, and, for those many who suffered uncontrollable diarrhoea, literally shat on."
– *Melissa Raphael*[111]

The German word *Scheiße*, meaning 'shit', was a guard's usual form of address to a Jew; corpses were referred to as *Scheiß-Stücke* (pieces of excrement). This was a catastrophe indeed; death before death, a long dying as the holy was systematically profaned. This is the purpose of sin: to ritually defile us until we can think of no worthwhile reason to live.

The opposite of catastrophe is 'euchatastrophe' – a word invented by the fantasy writer J.R.R. Tolkien to describe a good upheaval, a eucharistic revolution. Something like it is described in this scene from *The Lord of the Rings*.

'Gandalf!' Sam said. 'I thought you were dead! But then I thought I was dead myself. Is everything sad going to come untrue? What's happened to the world?'

'A great Shadow has departed', said Gandalf, and then he laughed, and the sound was like music, or like water in a parched land; and as he listened the thought came to Sam that he had not heard laughter, the pure sound of merriment, for days upon days without count. It fell upon his ears like the echo of all the joys he had ever known. But he himself burst into tears. Then, as a sweet

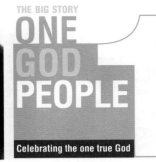

rain will pass down a wind of spring and the sun will shine out the clearer, his tears ceased, and his laughter welled up, and laughing he sprang from his bed.

'How do I feel?' he cried. 'Well, I don't know how to say it. I feel, I feel' – he waved his arms in the air – 'I feel like spring after winter, and sun on the leaves; and like trumpets and harps and all the songs I have ever heard.'  *– J.R.R. Tolkien, The Return of the King*[112]

**Holiness is not a dreary, morbid state, but is rather like pure, clean water; it is a refreshing delight, a true euchatastrophe.**

Being genuinely and substantially different requires thought, support, teaching and kind confrontation: when that happens, we become distinctive, not because we are *acting* differently but because we are being *transformed*, and are among those who are truly, spectacularly alive.

## Teaching Block 3:

# Looking closer: Shalom, Righteousness and Justice

"He has showed you, O man, what is good. And what does the LORD require of you? To act justly and to love mercy and to walk humbly with your God." *– Micah 6:8*

"I hate, I despise your religious feasts; I cannot stand your assemblies. Even though you bring me burnt offerings and grain offerings, I will not accept them. Though you bring choice fellowship offerings, I will have no regard for them. Away with the noise of your songs! I will not listen to the music of your harps. But let justice roll on like a river, righteousness like a never-failing stream!" *– Amos 5:21–24*

Both *personal and corporate holiness* are vital in the histories and prophets. Corporate holy living by the people of God was the primary concern of the priestly and prophetic traditions, and the primary concern of

the wisdom tradition was individual holy living. The Psalmist calls those who will 'ascend the hill of the Lord' to be committed to purity in *personal worship* and integrity in *corporate relationships*.

"Who shall ascend the hill of the LORD? And who shall stand in his holy place? He who has clean hands and a pure heart, who does not lift up his soul to what is false, and does not swear deceitfully." *– Psalm 24:2–3*

"[The Greek word for righteousness] *dikaiosune* and its Hebrew equivalent *sedeq* have something to do with personal piety, but everything to do with living a life which is in accord with the standard of justice set by God. This standard does not just involve the way we live our personal lives. It involves the way we react with the society in which we live. Isaiah 58 makes it clear that our lives should be based on justice – upon values which bring liberation for the oppressed and release the chains of injustice."

*– Peter Phillips*[113]

"Social ethics must never be substituted for personal ethics. Crusading can easily become a dodge for facing up to one's lack of personal morality. By the same token, even if I am a model of personal righteousness, that does not excuse my participation in social evil. The man who is faithful to his wife while he excuses bigotry towards his neighbour is no better than the adulterer who crusades for social justice. **What God requires is justice both personal and social.**"

*– R.C. Sproul*[114]

This twin call did not come as a progressive, enlightened way forward, but was rooted in the foundation of Israel and in the very character of the 'middle C' God himself.

## On solid rock

"I, the Lord, love justice."

*– Isaiah 61:8*

God is just; he calls for justice. A favourite Old Testament term for God is *the rock*, a symbol of stability and consistency (Deut 32:4). When God introduced the call to holiness to his people, it was a call to a personal and social ethic that included caring for the poor (Lev 19:2), caring for the elderly, looking after those with disabilities, feeding the poor, caring for the marginalized, and doing business with honesty – a call that reflected his own dependable character.

"The Lord of all the earth does justice…. It is an unrelinquishable affirmation of biblical faith – an affirmation that brings all parts of the Old Testament with its many streams of tradition into a unity – that is that he determines the right, upholds and establishes it, and rules the world of history by it. He is the Lord of the right."

*– James Muilenburg*[115]

"To walk in the ways of the Lord is the summary of Old Testament ethics."

*– Chris Wright*[116]

**Just as shalom is a rich word that speaks of everyone living under their own fig tree, so the word 'righteousness' – which speaks of straightness and faithfulness – is the command that we live rightly, in right relationship with all of creation. The New English Bible translates it as 'to see right prevail'.**

The root word for righteousness (*tsdq*) is used to describe pathways that are straight (Psa 23:3) and weights and measures that are correct (Lev 19:36, Deut 25:15). God is also the judge (*spt*) who arbitrates, makes judgements, and defends the legal rights of the oppressed. But this is no stern, impersonal rigidity: God is just because he loves. His justice is rooted in his faithfulness (*hesed*), or solid, steadfast loving-kindness. He is the truth (*emeth*) and therefore is stable and trustworthy. And his word is firm and trustworthy, because faithfulness also includes *emunah* – from which we get our word 'amen'.

The prophets further develop the priestly belief expressed in the Pentateuch that the holiness of God demands social justice (Isa 5:16; Jer 31:31–34; Ezek 28:22; 38:23). God manifests his holiness by moving humans to righteous living, by which they model his values in their communal life and mediate a true knowledge of the Holy One to the nations (Isa 42:1,6). God will not hear the prayers of those who ignore the cries of the poor (Isa 1:10–17). Caring for the poor sits at the very heart of what it genuinely means to know the Lord, and is therefore true religion – as in the case of King Josiah, described by the prophet Jeremiah and picked up later by James in the New Testament.

"'He defended the cause of the poor and needy, and so all went well. Is that not what it means to know me?' declares the LORD."

*– Jeremiah 22:16*

"Religion that God our Father accepts as pure and faultless is this: to look after orphans and widows in their distress and to keep oneself from being polluted by the world."

*– James 1:27*

"Concern for the poor is not merely an ethical teaching – it is first of all a theological truth, a central doctrine of the creed, a constantly repeated biblical teaching about the God we worship. The biblical insistence on God's concern for the poor is first of all a theological statement about the Creator and Sovereign of the universe."
– *Ronald Sider*[117]

"Among Israel's neighbours, as indeed in most ancient cultures of the world (including Indian, Chinese, African and South American civilizations), the power of the gods was channelled through the power of certain males – the priests, kings and warriors embodied divine power. Opposition to them was tantamount to rebellion against the gods. But… in Israel's rival vision, it is the 'orphan, the widow and the stranger' with whom Yahweh takes his stand. His power is exercised in history for their empowerment."
– *Vinoth Ramachandra*[118]

**In the histories, justice is demanded for the oppressed.**

- NATHAN CONFRONTS KING David about his treatment of poor Uriah (2 Sam 12:7).
- ELIJAH CHALLENGES KING Ahab and Jezebel for the way that they snatch Naboth's vineyard away (I Kings 21).
- THE WISDOM LITERATURE similarly calls for justice (Prov 16:12, 31:4, Eccl 5:8).
- JOB INITIALLY FELT that his troubles were undeserved because he had cared for the poor.

"If I have denied the desires of the poor or let the eyes of the widow grow weary, if I have kept my bread to myself, not sharing it with the fatherless—but from my youth I reared him as would a father, and from my birth I guided the widow—if I have seen anyone perishing for lack of clothing, or a needy man without a garment, and his heart did not bless me for warming him with the fleece from my sheep, if I have raised my hand against the fatherless, knowing that I had influence in court, then let my arm fall from the shoulder, let it be broken off at the joint. For I dreaded destruction from God, and for fear of his splendour I could not do such things."
– *Job 31:13–23*

Sadly, righteous men like Job were all too rare in Israel's history. In a gloomy play on words, the prophet Isaiah shows what God called for from his people and what they actually did.

"And he looked for justice (*mishpat*) but saw bloodshed (*mishpach*); for righteousness (*tsedaqah*), but heard cries of distress (*tseaqah*)."
– *Isaiah 5:7*

This understanding of God's justice leads some to suggest that the frequently used phrase 'God is biased towards the poor' is actually unhelpful. Rather, they say, God is utterly impartial. He sides neither with the rich nor the poor; but his loving attention is seized and his love aroused when he sees oppression and injustice. The poor are not excused for their sins, but are judged like everyone else (Isa 9:14–17) – including those who exploit them in their poverty.

"This undoubted fact of God's active concern for the weak and the poor needs to be expressed carefully. It is not a case of biased or arbitrary partiality on God's part, such as the expression, 'God is on the side of the poor' rather implies… rather, this group in society receives God's special attention because they are the wronged side of a situation of chronic injustice which God abhors and wishes to have redressed."
– *Chris Wright*[119]

"It is not that God is prejudiced in some way, still less that the poor are more deserving because of their poverty. Rather, because he is a God of justice, God opposes those who perpetuate injustice and he sides with the victims of oppression."
– *Tim Chester*[120]

"In a sinful world where life is biased towards the wealthy and the powerful, God's actions will always be perceived as a counter-bias." – *Vinoth Ramachandra*[121]

**Others, like David Sheppard, would suggest that 'bias to the poor' is a helpful phrase, because God's justice causes him to bend over backwards in favour of the poor.**

Jim Wallis supplies a graphic illustration of just how much the Bible has to say about the poor. A seminary student took a Bible and used a pair of scissors to cut out every reference to the poor.

"When the seminarian was finished that old Bible hung in threads. It wouldn't hold together, it fell apart in our hands. This is our Bible – full of holes from all that we have cut out."
– *Jim Wallis*[122]

## Holiness and harnessing youthful imagination

Yoweri Museveni became president of Uganda in 1986, when his National Resistance Army overthrew the military junta. Museveni had attended Christian youth camps during his teenage years, and while at one of the camps had asked that an evening be devoted to prayer for nearby Tanzania, which at the time was engaged in terrible civil war. He was told his request was inappropriate: 'We don't concern ourselves with things like that.' Prayers were said, but they focused on the needs of the camp and the spiritual well-being of those attending the event. Museveni made a decision: Christianity apparently had nothing to say about the needs of the day, so he would look elsewhere for a guiding philosophy for real life. He rejected a 'holiness' message that was a tragic misrepresentation; holiness has justice at its very heart.

**A message of holiness that is not holistic is doomed, for it will fail to capture the imaginations of our children.** And when that happens, we are impoverished.

"Children can provide the message of hope in a poor community."
– *Nora Avarientos, a development practitioner in the Philippines*[123]

In a Compassion UK (www.compassionuk.org) project in Ethiopia, children formerly sponsored from the West have set up their own sponsorship program in their village and raised money to support fellow students.[124] In Barranquilla, Colombia, child victims of domestic violence have painted a series of 'posters' on a mud wall in a prominent location in the village: each one represents the rights of a child.[125] In the Philippines, children's groups have organized a campaign against alcoholism and other addictions, and one children's group stood up in a public meeting and told the local politicians to stop being corrupt.[126] The dreams of children can transform communities.

Sarone Ole Sena of World Vision (www.worldvision.org.uk) Tanzania encourages children to articulate their dreams as they begin school. He insists that their dreams are part of the community's dream, and has found that children often have the capacity to dream 'bigger' than adults. In one remote Tanzanian village, children set out a dream for the year 2020 where every child would be educated; where no children died because of diarrhoea, measles or the flu; where adults and children worked together for the good of the community; and the community had healthy children for the next generation.[127]

Only a message that gives hope to the poor can have any potential for 'winning' our children. Otherwise the message of holiness, as Pete Broadbent says, becomes 'faintly and quaintly irrelevant'. Even worse, a distorted message of the gospel that does not include justice can cost lives.

## Bad theology costs lives: Rwanda

Bad theology truly costs lives. Rwanda is perhaps the bloodiest example of a nation that has undergone a 'revival' of piety that was socially disconnected – with horrendous results. Their tragic story is a warning to us all in the worldwide family of the church.

Rwanda was one of Africa's most evangelized countries, with over 80% of the population claiming to be Christian in the 1990s. During a revival in the 1930s, widespread conviction of sin, public confession and evangelism had spread across Uganda, South Africa, Kenya, Tanzania, Burundi and the Congo, as well as Rwanda. There had also

been some impact on ethnic issues, especially the attitudes of white missionaries; a favourite saying of the day was 'the ground is level at the Cross'.

## There are more slaves today than when the transatlantic slave trade was abolished.

But the teaching of the church was narrow and pietistic – focused on blessing, experiences and 'spiritual' concerns. It had failed to teach the lordship of Christ over all of life. When an aircraft carrying the Rwandan president was shot down in April 1994, unprecedented violence broke out between the Hutus and Tutsis. An estimated one million people were butchered in the ensuing slaughter. The church had taught a narrow understanding of the nature of sin that centred on private morality – lying, drinking, smoking, adultery. There was often unquestioning and naive support of those in power.

"One of the problems was lack of teaching on how the Scriptures could be applied to social and practical questions…. Some missionaries taught that politics was a dirty game and the Christian duty was to escape it." – *Emmanuel Kolini, Archbishop of Rwanda*[128]

"There was a need to know how to live out Christian discipleship in the secular world…. There was little awareness of the solidarities of sin that we are embedded in as members of society…. Missionaries preached a form of pietism that encouraged withdrawal from the public life of the nation or a naïve, uncritical support of the party in power." – *Roger Bowen, Mid-Africa Mission (formerly Rwandan Mission now part of Church Mission Society* www.cms-uk.org*)*[129]

"In the light of Rwanda, the most Christian nation in Africa, blowing up the way it did, does this reflect on Christian missionaries from the West offering 'cheap grace' which has not actually converted racial bias, the feelings of ethnic superiority, or the long held grudges of one people against another?" – *Alan Nichols*[130]

Misunderstanding what holiness is denies a vital truth that sits at the heart of all biblical revelation; and, as the tragedy of Rwanda reminds us, can have huge social consequences. How will we respond to the massive social injustices that are all around us? Holiness demands a response, whatever the personal cost. Three initiatives led by Christians focus on bringing God's justice to the critical issues of environmentalism, connecting the church to serve her community, and halting the multi-billion pound industry that is human trafficking.

## Christians engaging with the issues: Climate Change and Community Connection

"The scientific debate about whether climate change is really happening is over – it is happening fast, and the evidence is overwhelming." – *Andy Atkins, Advocacy Director of Tearfund* (www.tearfund.org)

"Climate change involves all of us as we share the same atmospheric resources. The question is, are we ready to give our lifestyles a critical look and see if we are causing damage to our neighbours and indeed the generation that is to come after us?" – *Tadesse Dadi, Tearfund Programme Support Advisor in Ethiopia*

Climate change is a key justice issue. Psalm 24 names the legal owner of the earth: 'The earth is the LORD's, and everything in it.' We are but tenants. Our misuse of what God has lent us is causing the planet to rapidly heat up. The world's poorest communities are feeling the greatest impact of climate change. As floods, droughts and storms increase, climate change threatens to create millions of 'environmental refugees'.

Every year, 150,000 people die as a direct result of climate change, according to the World Health Organisation. In Africa alone, 182 million people will die by the end of the century unless urgent action is taken by governments and citizens worldwide.

Tearfund's Tadesse Dadi recalls a conversation with an 82-year-old Ethiopian farmer, Mr Mengesha, who said that 30 years ago his harvest would last him two years, but now erratic rains mean his sons barely harvest enough to last them seven months. Around the world, the churches Tearfund works with report similar stories.

Tearfund's free booklet *For Tomorrow Too* gives simple, practical tips on how we can cut our carbon emissions – copies are available from Tearfund at Spring Harvest, from enquiry@tearfund.org or by calling 0845 355 8355. Visit www.tearfund.org/springharvest to find out more about climate change.

**The call for justice demands that we care for God's creation, and engage with the world at large and with our local and national communities.**

"I'm not a politician, nor am I an economist. I'm a pastor. I see the results of public policies on society and on the family…. The regeneration of our communities is an absolute priority … and that regeneration has got to be not just economic. It's got to be spiritual and moral, too." – *James Jones, the bishop of Liverpool*

As the social commentators and historians look back on the first years of the third millennium, they will record that these were the years of the slow, painful re-invention of public services in the UK.

There is a growing recognition that though the state can do many things well, it cannot deliver the personal or spiritual support we all need to overcome life's greatest adversities and to thrive.

In every community – rural, suburban and urban – there is an aching need for a fresh approach to tackle besetting needs. This means that the door of opportunity is wide open for every local church with a passion for justice, a commitment to bring God's shalom or well-being to community, and an appetite to get involved.

**People trafficking is the fastest growing global crime. Half the victims are children.**

**Faithworks** is a movement of thousands of individuals, churches and organisations motivated by their Christian faith to serve the needs of their local communities and positively influence society as a whole.

Faithworks works to:

- INSPIRE, RESOURCE AND equip local churches and individual Christians to develop their role at the hub of their community serving unconditionally.
- CHALLENGE AND CHANGE the public perception of the church by positively engaging with both government and media.
- ENCOURAGE PARTNERSHIP THAT avoids unnecessary competition and builds collaboration.

Faithworks equips churches and individuals to serve their local communities professionally. The Faithworks training programme is designed to help a local church move to the next level of engagement with its community. For more information visit www.faithworks.info

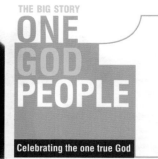

## Wilberforce and slavery: Stop The Traffik

William Wilberforce was one of the tireless leaders of the emancipation of slaves movement in the 19th century. Wilberforce was part of the Clapham Sect, a group of like minded 'serious' Christians, possibly influenced by Calvinism, who included Henry Thornton of Battersea Rise in Clapham.

The campaign he led in Parliament against the British slave trade lasted 20 years until its triumph in 1807. The abolition of slavery itself took another 27 years. Wilberforce is chiefly remembered as one of the parliamentarians who eventually secured the freedom of African slaves after a huge struggle with landed interests and the planters abroad, particularly in Jamaica.

**There are more slaves today than when the transatlantic slave trade was abolished in the 19th century.**

Two hundred years after Wilberforce and others fought to abolish the trans-Atlantic slave trade, people trafficking remains a global problem. It affects every continent, and most countries. Due to the hidden and illegal nature of human trafficking, gathering statistics on the scale of the problem is a complex and difficult task. Here is a conservative estimate.

- AT LEAST 12.3 million people are victims of forced labour.
- 2.4 MILLION OF these are as a result of human trafficking.
- 1.2 MILLION CHILDREN are trafficked each year.
- 500,000 WOMEN WERE trafficked into the EU in 1995.
- BETWEEN 142 AND 1,420 women a year are trafficked into and within the UK for sexual exploitation.
- 250 CHILD TRAFFICKING cases were uncovered in the UK between 1987 and 2001.
- 35 CHILD TRAFFICKING cases were found in 17 London boroughs in 2003.

Spring Harvest is a member of Stop The Traffik, a global coalition, covering over 40 countries, working to stop people trafficking – the buying and selling of people around the world.

Stop The Traffik's call is:
- **PREVENT THE SALE OF PEOPLE**
- **PROSECUTE THE TRAFFICKERS**
- **PROTECT THE VICTIMS**

People trafficking is the fastest growing global crime, affecting every continent. It is one of the three largest illegal trades alongside arms and drugs. It is a global industry worth over seven billion dollars a year. Men, women and children are all victims of trafficking; although approximately 80% are women and girls, and around 50% are children.

Stop The Traffik is working in three areas:
- **EDUCATION**: CREATING AWARENESS and understanding of the subject, capturing people's imaginations and inspiring them to act.
- **ADVOCACY**: SHOWING PEOPLE how they can make a difference and helping put pressure on authorities and governments to take action.
- **FUNDRAISING**: TO FINANCE new projects by organisations working with trafficked people across the world, e.g. safe houses and vocational training.

At the end of 2007 The Stop The Traffik Declaration, hopefully signed by millions of people around the world, will be delivered to the United Nations, and copied to local governments.

To find out more or to join Stop The Traffik, either as an individual or an organisation, visit www.stopthetraffik.org

## So what? Person to Person: For individual reflection

### 'Is this what you do with eternity?'

Groundhog Day is the story of Phil Connors, played by Bill Murray. Connors is a self-centred, sarcastic television weatherman who covers the annual Groundhog Day Celebration in Punxsutawney, Pennsylvania. Connors despises the whole event, believing it to be unworthy of his time. After filming his piece to camera, Connors and his producer, Rita (Andie MacDowell), are caught in a giant blizzard (which he failed to predict) and are forced to stay in town. When he wakes up the next day, however, something very strange has happened – it's February 2 all over again – and the next morning, and every morning thereafter. Connors comes to believe that whatever he does, there will be no consequences – it will always be February 2 – and so he throws himself into crime, materialism, money and sex, all of which leaves him unfulfilled. He falls for Rita, but can't manipulate her to love him back, and finally says (in what sounds amazingly like a pre-conversion statement): 'I've come to the end of me. There's no way out now.' But Phil commits suicide – only to wake up on February 2 once more. Life is forever the same.

Connors confides in Rita and tells her what's going on. As he speaks, he tosses cards into a hat, and she asks, 'Is this what you do with eternity?'

Realizing that life is not just about idle play, Connors turns to art, poetry, music and sculpture. He pours himself into serving the community he despised, Punxsutawney. He reaches out, comes to really know and be known, and is finally fulfilled: he is reborn.[131]

Are we frittering eternity away, with every day following the same track as the one before? Ask yourself, How would God have me change my mind? Is he calling me to reorient my priorities or make a cataclysmic change for the better, even though the change seems incredibly risky? What would it mean for me to more fully embrace and express his holistic holiness?

## Suggested reading

**Holiness past and present** – Stephen Barton (editor), Conti

NOT FOR THE faint hearted, this series of contributions from different scholars clears the fog about authentic holy living for today.

**Walking with the poor** – Bryant L. Myers, Alban

CHALLENGING PRINCIPLES AND practicalities. Calling us to play our part in world transformation. A synthesis of theology, spirituality and social science.

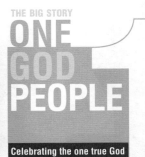

## So what? People to People: For group discussion together

### Reflect on Gerard Kelly's prayer:

I want my heart
To be willing to make house-calls.
Let those whose rope is at an end
Find in me a faithful friend,
Let me be known as one who re-builds broken walls.

Share how your church is being a faithful friend to those in your community who are at the end of their rope. What would you say to people from a church that has never really connected with its communities needs – how can they make a start?

### Stop The Traffik responses:

Is your church part of Stop The Traffik and if so how are you involved?

What could your church do to be involved in Stop The Traffik?

- IDEAS:
  - raising awareness
  - building the petition
  - supporting a project
  - educating your members and the community
  - putting pressure on power brokers (local MP, national government, EU, UN)

What were the personal values William Wilberforce and his friends exemplified in their lives and work, and what challenges did they have to overcome in the fight for justice?

- WHO DO YOU think are the modern day equivalents of William Wilberforce?
  1. in the world

  2. in your community

  3. in the church

  4. in your church

**Can slavery ever be eradicated?**

# 4 ONE PEOPLE: IN THE LIFE OF JESUS

CATHOLIC

One Holy, **Catholic**, Apostolic People

When a **Samaritan woman** came to draw water, Jesus said to her, "Will you give me a drink?" (His disciples had gone into the town to buy food.)

The **Samaritan woman** said to him, "You are a **Jew** and I am a **Samaritan woman**. How can you ask me for a drink?" (**For Jews do not associate with Samaritans.**)

Jesus answered her, "If you knew the **gift of God** and who it is that asks you for a drink, you would have asked him and he would have given you living water." – *John 4:7–10*

# 4 ONE PEOPLE: IN THE LIFE OF JESUS

Today's goal – explore how the book of John takes on the format of a creation story (a re-creation story). To understand the impact this theological insight has on the ministry of Jesus, and its effect on us in our thinking and practice.

## Teaching Block 1:

### To the Boundaries and Margins: Jesus for all

Teaching Block 1: If Jesus takes the broadest view of who the people of God are, then how does that impact how we are church and how we do church?

We shall explore the terminology of 'sinner' alongside the understanding that Jesus spent so much of his time with 'sinners' and contrast it to the understanding of the Pharisees.

We shall consider what impact this has on our thinking and attitudes. We shall look at how are we to encourage the same revolution that Jesus began in his building of a catholic church in relation to women and children.

## Teaching Block 2:

### The Message of the Kingdom: It's Sunday, but Monday's Coming

Teaching Block 2: We are going to learn about the term 'the kingdom of God', looking at the Jewish understanding, Jesus' declaration and its impact on our message.

We shall investigate the distinction between the kingdom and the church and how these relate to the term 'the people of God'. We'll explore the concept of the kingdom of God through the text in order to discover new ways in which the church is to be a signpost to it.

## Teaching Block 3:

### One Catholic Church in a Fragmented World

Teaching Block 3: We shall discover what a unified global church looks like and what we can do to respond to this. We'll be looking at how we discover/know that God is at work and how this is linked to the work of the people of God and the presence of the church. It's a chance to look through some of the windows of opportunity for moving out of our comfort zones and towards a truer catholic unity in action with black majority churches and persecuted churches.

# One Holy Catholic People – the People of God in the life and ministry of Jesus

# Introduction

## Prelude: A well and living water

The woman would have been surprised, and probably uncomfortable, at the presence of a stranger. She was probably a social leper among her own people, the Samaritans, because of the gaggle of men that she'd been involved with. Perhaps that's why she went to the well to draw water when she did. She picked the hour of the day when the sun rode highest in the sky, and sensible people stayed out of the relentless heat. Usually the place would have been deserted; but not today. He was a Jew. The best she could hope for was stony silence – but there might be bruising, abusive words. Jews considered Samaritan women to have begun their 'unclean' menstrual cycle at birth.

Imagine her further surprise when he warmly initiated a conversation, asking for her help. 'Can I have a drink?' Jews and Samaritans didn't talk – and to share an eating or drinking utensil was completely unthinkable. But then he was ignoring all social propriety by talking publicly with a woman. Her eyes grew wide as he spoke about living water, and about a time to come when the people of God would not lay claim to any ethnic pedigree, or any special place of worship; it wouldn't matter *who* you were, or *where* you were. The issue was not whether you worshipped on Mount Gerazim in the ruins of an old temple, as the Samaritans held it, or in Jerusalem at the magnificent temple there, as the Jews insisted.

But Jesus talked of a day when women and men and children everywhere, in every distant corner of the earth, would know the call to worship in spirit and in truth. God was out looking for worshippers like this – a universal banquet. And suddenly, stunningly, she found herself on the guest list. He spoke of living water that could soothe *her* parched lips. Her mind struggled – was he talking about magic liquid? And then this kind stranger knew all about her shame, but still talked about her enjoying eternal life. Only Messiah could say such things, and she told him so. And that's when he said it: 'I who speak to you am he.'

In the short story *The Woman at the Well* by Gary Swanson, the woman is described returning to her lover, flushed with excitement, having met Jesus. She tells him that she's met Messiah, but he's not convinced. How can she bump into Messiah during such a tedious domestic duty like fetching water? And how does she know that this is who the stranger is?

"'It seems he knows us better than we do ourselves. He knows what we want – what we really want.'

'What do we really want?'

'You will know that when you see him.'

'I am not a religious man...'

She took his hand and led him to the door. 'That is just the part that is the most thrilling – neither is he.'[132]

Because of her meeting with Jesus, a new and remarkable 'church' in Samaria is born, gifted with the knowledge of the universal nature of the ministry of Jesus, who had come to redeem Israel, but not just Israel.

"They said to the woman, 'We no longer believe just because of what you said; now we have heard for ourselves, and we know that this man really is the Saviour of the world.'" – John 4:42

New life – the opportunity to become a new creation – is available to *all* in Christ.

## I make all things new

In Mel Gibson's celebrated and controversial film, *The Passion of the Christ*, a poignant scene (birthed in Gibson's imagination but rooted in Revelation 21:5) unfolds when Jesus stumbles as he drags his cross along the Via Dolorosa. Mary, her heart shattered by the agony of a mother watching her child go to his execution, rushes to help him to his feet, and as she does, she remembers a moment when he'd had a childhood scrape, and how she had tenderly helped him and nursed his bruised knees. And then Jesus and Mary share a final, private moment; his face bloodied and pulverized, Jesus gasps just one sentence to her, a few words that reveal the reason for the agony that they share: 'You see, Mother, I'm making all things new!'

As John records the story of Jesus and the woman at the well, he points to the Christ who was doing far more than coming to earth to clean us up and get us ready for eternity.

Along with the other Gospel writers, he is pointing to a whole new order of things, where outsiders are in, where those who smugly believe themselves to be at the epicentre of God's purposes suddenly find they have excluded themselves from the party; where the 'experts' are the fools, and the children are the wise ones; where

angels visit shepherds (a traditionally despised occupation), where women are called as resurrection witnesses (unthinkable in a courtroom of those days), and where tax collectors, despised by all as traitors and collaborators, become part of the Jesus team.

But there's even more, because the Gospel of John is a 'Genesis' type of document that describes an act of creation. Any Jewish reader would connect with the opening words, 'In the beginning was the Word' (John 1:1), and know that this was a book about creation. And indeed it is, for Jesus comes to create a new humanity, a people so radically different from the 'old style' human beings that they would describe their experience as like being born again.

And he creates a new community through the work of the Cross, a people living under the loving reign of the Royal Family that is the Trinity. This is a community that crosses every human boundary and barrier; they are the people of God, a people made up from people everywhere.

In the first creation, Adam and Eve were the people of God – but they became estranged by the fall. In Christ, the invitation to God's banquet is extended to everyone, everywhere. In a broken world God calls the whole of humanity to become God's people.[133]

"Therefore, if anyone is in Christ, he is a new creation; the old has gone, the new has come!" – 2 Corinthians 5:17

N.T. Wright[134] points out that the parallels between Genesis and John continue.

- ON THE SIXTH day of the week, God makes humanity in his image (Gen 1:26); on Friday, the sixth day, Jesus stands before Pilate, who affirms, 'Here is the man' (John 19:5).
- AT THE END of the sixth day, God finished the work he had done (Gen 2:1); Jesus cries 'It is finished!' on the evening of the sixth day (John 19:30).

- ON THE SEVENTH day, God rested (Gen 2:2); Jesus rested in the tomb on the seventh day (John 19:42).
- ON THE FIRST day of week, while it was still dark (John 20:1), Christ arose, life and order bursting forth into swirling chaos, just like Creation Day (Gen 1:2). Wright points out that Mary mistook Jesus for the gardener (John 20:15); with all these overtones of Eden, in a sense he was and is.
- JESUS BREATHES UPON the gathered disciples (John 20:22), just as God breathed life into the nostrils of humanity (Gen 2:7). **The 'new creation' species is born: any and all can now receive light and new life in his name: truly a 'catholic' church, if we properly understand the use of that term.**

## Defining the term 'catholic'

When we use the word 'catholic', and affirm in the creed that we are part of one holy *catholic* apostolic church, we are using a word that means 'universal' – the word is derived from the Greek adjective καθολικός (*katholikos*). **We are declaring that all Christians everywhere, from every era, irrespective of race, nationality or gender, form a single united group, which is the body of Christ** (1 Cor 12:27).

Saint Ignatius of Antioch was the earliest known writer to use the phrase 'catholic church' and he used it in particular to define orthodox biblical faith over against heterodox beliefs.

Vincent of Lerins defines catholic faith as '*quod ubique, quod semper, quod ab omnibus credituni est*' (that which has been believed everywhere, always, by everyone) – a uniting and easy definition, but one that is more difficult to pin down in detail.

Both the Roman Catholic Church and the Eastern Orthodox Church believe that the phrase 'one holy catholic' in the Nicene Creed calls for a visible *institutional* unity, not only throughout the world *organizationally*, but also down the centuries in terms of *apostolic succession*. As they see it,

unity is one of the four marks that the creed attributes to the church, and the essence of a mark is that it be visible.

Similarly, some Anglicans and Lutherans view unity as a mark of catholicity, but see the institutional unity of the catholic church manifested in the shared apostolic succession of their episcopacies.

Generally Evangelical Christians hold that the 'one holy catholic and apostolic church' refers to the 'true' church of Christ as the communion of saints (i.e. those who have been saved through divine grace).

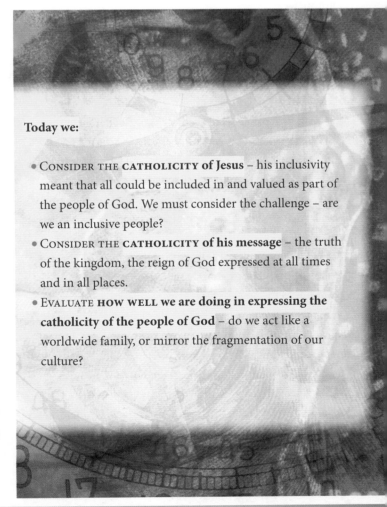

**Today we:**

- CONSIDER THE **CATHOLICITY of Jesus** – his inclusivity meant that all could be included in and valued as part of the people of God. We must consider the challenge – are we an inclusive people?
- CONSIDER THE **CATHOLICITY of his message** – the truth of the kingdom, the reign of God expressed at all times and in all places.
- EVALUATE **HOW WELL we are doing in expressing the catholicity of the people of God** – do we act like a worldwide family, or mirror the fragmentation of our culture?

## Teaching Block 1:

# To the boundaries and margins: Jesus for all

**Jesus had the broadest vision of what and who the people of God are. His teaching and lifestyle demonstrated his catholicity.**

### Inside outsiders

Right from the start, it was obvious that Jesus had embarked on a mission that would enable 'outsiders' in the culture to become kingdom 'insiders'. God revealed his birth to astrologers in the East and shepherds on the hills. Sheep tending was considered to be a dishonest, dirty trade because shepherds often trespassed. They would lead their flocks onto land to which they had no legal right. They would sell the milk and lambs, but pocket the money rather than passing it on to their employers. No wonder some rabbis taught that sheep herding was a disreputable occupation.[135] Yet Jesus called himself 'the good shepherd' (John 10:11,14). His use of this title is rooted in imagery common in the ancient Near East of rulers as shepherds. Pharaohs, for example, carried a small shepherd's crook as part of their regalia. In particular, when Jesus calls himself the good shepherd he is picking up on Ezekiel 34, where God speaks of himself as the true shepherd of Israel.

And when it comes to birth announcements, it's the women who believe (and who, as we'll see, were considered second class citizens) and the men who doubt, e.g. Mary and Zechariah (Luke 1:12-21, cf. Luke 1:38). Simeon caught a glimpse of the catholicity of Jesus' mission.

"For my eyes have seen your salvation, which you have prepared in the sight of all people, *a light for revelation to the Gentiles* and for glory to your people Israel." – *Luke 2:30–32 (emphasis added)*

Fishermen enjoyed moderate respect, and carpentry was an esteemed trade, but Jesus spent most of his time with demoniacs, prostitutes, tax collectors and adulterers, as well as people tragically stigmatised because they were blind, deaf, disabled, diseased or lepers. These people were seen as social throwaways – but not by Jesus. Society was divided into rigid boxes, but Jesus refused to acknowledge this categorisation. He actively worked to undermine and overthrow such prejudicial thinking.

"**The spirit of Jesus penetrates social boxes. Barricades of suspicion, mistrust, stigma and hate crumble in his presence. He calls us to see the human being behind the stigmatised social labels. His kingdom transcends all boundaries. He welcomes people from all boxes. His love overpowers the social customs which divide, separate and isolate. … The agape of Jesus reaches out to boxed-up people, telling them God's love washes away their stigma and welcomes them into a new community.**" – *Donald Kraybill*[136]

The makeup of his team points to Jesus' catholicity. There we find Matthew, formerly one of the hated tax collectors

(Luke 5:28), serving alongside Simon the Zealot (Luke 6:15), who in other circumstances would have wanted to plant a dagger between Matthew's shoulders. It is also notable that while some of the twelve have Hebrew/Aramaic names Philip and Andrew have Greek names, reflecting a cultural spectrum within Judaism of the time. **Jesus' team came from opposite ends of the political spectrum to be members of the group that walked with him. His unfolding ministry reached out to embrace those considered unworthy of the time of day, and this merits a closer look.**

## Gentiles at the party

We saw on Day Two that God elected Israel as his people for the sake of *all* peoples – a lighthouse for the nations. In the early pages of the books of Moses, the Gentiles receive a divine blessing. By the time of Jesus, that vision has not only almost totally disappeared but been replaced by an attitude of ethnic superiority. Gentiles are now called 'wild dogs'.

So-called ethnic purity was very important in Jesus' day – a clean 'pedigree' was required to engage in court or hold public office; a 'pure' family tree was a ticket to power and influence.

The pecking order was as follows:

1. PRIESTS, LEVITES AND others of pure lineage.

2. SLIGHTLY BLEMISHED JEWS, like the illegitimate offspring of priests, and proselytized Jews.

3. OTHER ILLEGITIMATE OFFSPRING, eunuchs and persons with unknown fathers.

4. CIRCUMCISED GENTILE SLAVES.

5. SAMARITANS AND GENTILES.

Overlaying this was a simpler order of rank – Jews come first and Gentiles most definitely come second.

The way that Jesus approached Gentiles is difficult to summarise, particularly when we read Matthew's Gospel. Written particularly for a Jewish audience, it treats Gentiles with far less sympathy. But even Matthew sees Jesus fulfilling the words of Isaiah, as the bringer of hope to all the nations.

> "Here is my servant whom I have chosen, the one I love, in whom I delight; I will put my Spirit on him, and he will proclaim justice to the nations. He will not quarrel or cry out; no one will hear his voice in the streets. A bruised reed he will not break, and a smouldering wick he will not snuff out, till he leads justice to victory. In his name the nations will put their hope." – *Matthew 12:18–21 (quoting Isa 42:1–4 in the Septuagint version)*

And elsewhere Jesus is shown to display a staggering, revolutionary openness to Gentiles. He operates in their territory, healing the sick, casting out demons and feeding

> **Jesus took his stand among the pariahs of his world. Sinners were his table companions.**

the 4,000. A Gentile woman affirms that Jesus is the Lord, in contrast to the blindness of the Jewish 'Hebrew of Hebrews' Pharisees. Jesus finds faith among the Gentiles, even in the heart of a Roman centurion. And in Matthew's Gospel, the staggering picture of a Gentile who 'gets it' about Jesus, in contrast to the blindness of the Jewish audience, is clear.

> "Truly I say to you, not even in Israel have I found such faith." – *Matthew 8:10*

This Gentile faith prompts Jesus to prophesy.

> "I say to you that many will come from the east and the west, and will take their places at the feast with Abraham, Isaac and Jacob in the kingdom of heaven. But the subjects of the kingdom will be thrown outside, into the darkness, where there will be weeping and gnashing of teeth."
> – *Matthew 8:11–12*

The Gerasene demoniac was a Gentile who ended up worshipping Jesus and calling him 'Son of the Most High God' (Mark 5:7). Jesus instructs the healed demoniac to tell his friends – obviously Gentiles – what God had done for him. **The followers of Jesus were to be the 'light of the** *world'* **and not just of Israel. The kingdom was breaking through the Jewish/Gentile barrier, and the 'sinners' got a special invitation to the party.**

## Supper with sinners and war with the Pharisees

> "Living the trinitarian faith means living as Jesus Christ lived; preaching the gospel; relying totally upon God; offering healing and reconciliation; rejecting laws, customs and conventions that place people beneath rules; resisting temptation; praying constantly; eating with modern day lepers and other outcasts; embracing the enemy and the sinner; dying for the sake of the gospel if it is God's will."
> – *Catherine Mowray LaCugna[137]*

As we saw yesterday, the Pharisees of Jesus' day have been vilified as the pantomime bad guys throughout Christian history. Modern scholarship has shown that they were, in many cases, passionate and committed people who were trying to integrate principles of holiness into everyday life. Not only had hypocrisy crept in, however, but they had drawn boundaries around the community of God that Jesus shattered with his continual habit of befriending sinners.

> "All the people saw this and began to mutter, 'He has gone to be the guest of a "sinner".'"
> – *Luke 19:7*

> "Now the tax collectors and 'sinners' were all gathering around to hear him. But the Pharisees and the teachers of the law muttered, 'This man welcomes sinners and eats with them.'"
> – *Luke 15:1–2*

> "Table fellowship was the central feature of Jesus' ministry."
> – *Norman Perrin[138]*

> "Jesus took his stand among the pariahs of his world, those despised by the respectable. Sinners were his table companions and the ostracised tax collectors and prostitutes his friends."
> – *Geza Vermes[139]*

There is confusion over the meaning of the word 'sinners' in the gospels because of our fluency with the truth, particularly expounded in Romans, that we are all sinners. A cursory review of Jesus' activity suggests he simply practised friendship and teaching with ordinary, everyday people. But in the first century, 'sinner' was a specific derogatory word used to describe outcasts and 'untouchables'.

Outcasts and untouchables were people who:

- PRACTISED ONE OF the 'seven despised trades'. They included tax collectors, barbers, tanners and shepherds.
- WERE CONSIDERED GUILTY of flagrant immorality, like prostitutes, adulterers, gamblers and murderers.
- DID NOT OBSERVE the law, according to the Pharisees' understanding of it.
- WERE GENTILES, WHO were excluded from the 'holiness reserved for Israel alone' – the 'Gentile sinners' (Mark 14:41, Gal 2:15).

> "He touched untouchables with love and washed the guilty clean." – *Communion Service, Common Worship[140]*

Notice it is said that Jesus was a friend of 'tax collectors and sinners' – tax gatherers as a group were especially singled out for mention. It was believed that if a tax collector entered any house, not only the food but the entire house was rendered unclean.[141] Some taught that repentance

was completely impossible for tax collectors,[142] who were seen as collaborators with the occupying forces, 'lackeys of Rome'[143] and a threat to the cohesion of the community's goal of holiness. No wonder there was such conflict when some of them became Jesus' friends.

> "Jesus' actions implied an acceptance of quisling behaviour and threatened to shatter the closed ranks of the community against their enemy and to break down the cohesiveness necessary to the survival of a society immersed in conflict."
> – Marcus Borg[144]

Jesus enjoyed 'table fellowship' with these sinners – just as we have considered the word 'sinner', we must briefly examine the significance of a shared meal in the first century. **In Near Eastern thinking, sitting at a table with someone was considered an act of intimacy and fellowship. To offer hospitality was to give honour[145] and trusting acceptance. Refusal to share a meal conversely signalled rejection and disapproval.**

> We must also allow ourselves to be challenged about our proximity to the world.

But the Pharisees took the idea of table fellowship further. Because they were radicals who wanted God's holiness to be expressed in every area of daily life, every meal became like an act of worship in the temple. They had 229 texts of regulations about table fellowship. Some scholars describe them as 'a table fellowship sect'.[146] All food had to have been subjected to tithing, and was carefully prepared with ritual hand washings. A meal could not be shared with anyone who might 'defile' it. Table fellowship for the first-century Jew also had a strong sense of eschatological hope at its

heart; the meal shared was a picture of the eternal shared banquet to come.

And there were political implications to table fellowship: it was a 'survival symbol'[147] for a people occupied by a hated force. **Jesus took the everyday practice of sharing a meal and made it a 'living parable' – and perhaps more, as he demonstrated the explosive catholicity of his mission.**

> "Jesus did not simply accept the central role of table fellowship, but used it as a weapon. From the fact that his teaching shows an awareness of the meal, it is clear that his action was deliberately provocative."
> – Marcus Borg[148]

> "This was [about] revolutionary action, protest, and the silencing of critics."
> – David Daube[149]

> "Disputes about table fellowship were not matters of genteel etiquette, but about the shape of the community whose life truly manifested loyalty to Yahweh."
> – Marcus Borg[150]

When attacked for his eating habits, Jesus gave a four-fold response.

- He refused to play religious games or submit to what some saw as orthodoxy (Luke 7:31–35) – a call to maturity.
- He saw 'sinners' as being like sick people in need of help and health with him as the doctor (Mark 2:15–17), a hint that table fellowship was part of the restorative process – a call to compassion.
- He insisted that those excluded by religion (like Zacchaeus the tax collector, designated as a gentile without hope) could be part of God's people as a 'son of Abraham' (Luke 19:7–10) – a call to hope for inclusivity.
- He taught that the homecoming of sinners is an event worth partying over (Luke 15:1–24) – a call to joy and generous welcome.

# 4 ONE PEOPLE: IN THE LIFE OF JESUS

More than forgiveness is being offered here. Jesus was essentially clarifying the nature of true holiness, and erasing some of the boundary lines that Pharisaic thinking had drawn around Israel.

"Jesus challenged the quest for holiness and replaced it with an alternative vision."
– *Marcus Borg*[151]

## Jesus was showing that authentic holiness is:

- **A POWERFUL POSITIVE FORCE that can change those it comes into contact with**; holiness does not need to be cloistered or protected. Far from being fragile, it is able to bring wholeness where there is brokenness and scatter the forces of darkness. The leper does not make Jesus unclean, but is cleansed by him (Mark 1:40–45); the Gerasene demoniac (Mark 5:1–20) is unclean for many reasons (he lives among tombs, in Gentile territory, near swine, and is possessed by an unclean spirit) yet he is cleansed by the power of Jesus' holy presence and the command of his word. The wonderful truth of the clean hallowing the unclean is continued in Paul's thinking about believers married to unbelievers, and the sanctifying effect of the Christian (1 Cor 7:12–14).

- **EXPRESSED IN 'RISKY' compassion**. The Good Samaritan (Luke 10:33,37), considered an unclean, despised heretic, is declared 'good': the cultural equivalent to Jewish ears of 'the Good Nazi'. The Samaritan's goodness is demonstrated by his caring and compassionate attitude. Jesus' listeners would have entirely expected the priest and Levite to 'pass by on the other side' because it would have made them unclean to be within four cubits of a dying or dead person; allowing your shadow to pass over a corpse or passing under the shadow of a rock that overhung a corpse also created uncleanness.[152] But a Jew was required to stop and help a fellow Jew who was in need of aid – which would have meant the priest and Levite having to take a risk. The Pharisaic thinking of the day would have applauded their passing by, rather than 'risk' defilement. **But Jesus challenged that thinking, teaching that it is better to take chances on the side of**

compassion than stay in the safety of personal cleanliness. Just as the father in the parable had 'compassion' on his lost son (Luke 15:20), Jesus calls for 'mercy, not sacrifice' (Matt 9:13) just as Hosea had (Hos 6:6).

- **COMPASSION SHOWN TO those currently outside Israel – or the covenant**. Jewish thinking was that God's covenant love was for God's covenant people – but God's love brings the sun and rain to the just and unjust. The law required the Jew to love his or her neighbour – which was interpreted to mean a fellow Jew – but Jesus dismissed that boundary thinking by demanding that we love our enemies (Matt 5:44).

- **IMITATING WHAT GOD the Father does** – what Borg calls the *imitatio dei* – and God welcomes sinners. We who have been reached out to must ourselves reach out – mercy has consequences.[153]

"Jesus says, in effect, 'God is your Father. Become what you are, his child. Like father, like child; to live as a child of God is to treat your neighbour as God treats you…; to imitate in one's behaviour the quality and direction of God's activity.' "
– *C.H. Dodd*[154]

Jesus' table fellowship habits perhaps call into question the sense of 'separated' community that is created by church membership. We must consider how well we deal with people who do not readily embrace biblical ethics coming into our church families. Is it possible that many churches welcome 'sinners' as long as they graduate from their sinful habits in a reasonably quick time period?

We must also allow ourselves to be challenged about our proximity to the wider world, the way that we spend our time and the friendships we invest in lest we see holiness as something that needs to be protected from the 'big bad' world, rather than a force for transformation that can change the world.

Gentiles and sinners were 'in'. And so were women and children – so often left outside.

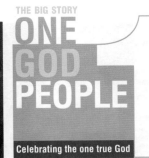
## Jesus and women

" Blessed be God that hath not made me a woman."
– *Jewish prayer offered daily by men in Jesus' day*[155]

" That great plank of the Reformation, the priesthood of all believers, sometimes appears to be believed to mean 'the priesthood of all white Anglo-Saxon English-speaking male believers'. But, in a family where God has broken down the dividing walls of ethnicity, social status and gender, and replaced that in Christ with an equality between different members of the family as sons and daughters, we need to think again – and with great humility – about how we are going to relate to one another with love and respect."        – *Rose Dowsett*[156]

Women in Jesus' day were subjected to the shackles of countless rules; one of the six major divisions of the Mishnah is devoted to rules exclusively pertaining to women, while there are no rules exclusively for men. There are seventy-two legal paragraphs about ritual uncleanness and menstruation. Their life was extremely hard.

- Women had no identity, having to cover themselves in veils whenever in public – so much so that, Marcus Borg records, a chief priest in Jerusalem, unaware of her identity, accused his own mother of adultery.
- They had no place in public life and could never be alone with a man not their husband. A woman could be divorced for talking with a man in the street.
- Daughters could be given in engagement by their fathers at the age of twelve, and married at thirteen, with the father of the bride receiving a large sum of money from his future son-in-law – so young girls were seen as a source of cheap labour and huge profit.
- A woman was really a slave in her own home, confined to domestic chores that included washing her husband's hands, face and feet.
- She was called to absolute obedience, like a Gentile slave.
- She had no right of divorce.

- Her ultimate achievement was the production of a male child, the birth of which was greeted with joy. Female children were received with dismay.
- Women could not study the law. They were forbidden to teach. (One teacher said it was better to burn the law than let a woman teach it.)
- Women could not pray at a meal or give evidence in a court – because they were generally considered to be liars. The Hebrew words for 'pious', 'just' and 'holy' do not have a feminine form.
- Women could not approach the Holy of Holies in the Temple, or even go into the Outer Courts, when they were menstruating.

> It is odd that parents' treatment of children is not a matter of global public concern.

It is against this background of oppression and injustice that we see just how revolutionary and inclusive Jesus was in his approach to women.

- Women became his followers and friends; Mary Magdalene, Joanna and Susanna were among those who accompanied him. He declared that female harlots would enter the kingdom before some righteous Jewish males (Matt 21:31). It is a woman who understands that Jesus is to die, and anoints him in advance for burial. He doesn't rebuke the woman with a never-ending period because she has touched his cloak, but blesses her (Mark 5:25–34).
- Luke in his gospel shows a special interest in the way Jesus approaches women, as he raises from dead the widow's son and saves her from becoming an object of

charity. The Martha and Mary story is not only about busyness, but also redefines the woman's domestic role in the home. Mary forgets the kitchen, enjoys the discussion and teaching – and is commended by Jesus for doing so (Luke 10:38–42). Women helped provide financial support for his work (Luke 8:1–3).

- WOMEN ARE AMONG the most loyal of Jesus' disciples in the gospels. While the men ran away when pressure hit (Mark 14:50), and even the males who felt like they would be faithful to Jesus to the end, like Peter, actually buckled, it was the women who witnessed the crucifixion in all four gospels (Matt 27:55, Mark 15:40, Luke 23:49, John 19:25).

- THE RESURRECTION WAS announced first to women, with Mary Magdalene being the first to Jesus alive again (John 20:11-18). Women are mocked by unbelieving men as they report the resurrection, and accused of spreading 'an idle tale' (Luke 24:11).

- JESUS USES FEMALE imagery to describe piety, and even the nature of God. It is the widow who gives sacrificially. God is likened to a female hen wanting to gather her chicks (Matt 23:37) and a woman looking for a coin (Luke 15:8–10).

"By word and by deed Jesus confers a new dignity on women. One confesses him as Lord. He reveals his messianic nature to another. And women, of all people, are chosen as the first witnesses of the resurrection. In a male-dominated culture these were powerful signs that women had a new status in the upside down kingdom."
– Donald Kraybill[157]

All of us, women and men, must ask ourselves if Jesus' catholicity is being expressed in the way women experience church in 2007. All of us must face up to the shackles placed on women that limit their contribution to the church's ministry.

Women and men must together consider how best the church can 'hear' the voices of women. Some who have been reluctant to put themselves forward must speak out while others must now take the time to listen

and encourage. We need to find ways to facilitate the integration of women into leadership contexts formerly dominated by men, with male team and communication styles.

There is a huge need in the British church for female Bible teachers and speakers, with some of the few in place feeling they have to adopt a male style in order to communicate. Action is required on all sides.

## Children matter

"He called a little child and had him stand among them. And he said: 'I tell you the truth, unless you change and become like little children, you will never enter the kingdom of heaven. Therefore, whoever humbles himself like this child is the greatest in the kingdom of heaven. And whoever welcomes a little child like this in my name welcomes me. But if anyone causes one of these little ones who believe in me to sin, it would be better for him to have a large millstone hung around his neck and to be drowned in the depths of the sea.'"
– Matthew 18:2–5

In Jesus' day, children had no status or power. They were totally dependent upon others, and easily brushed aside by the disciples of Jesus who saw them as social nobodies with nothing to offer in terms of advancing the kingdom cause. They were seen as a time-consuming distraction, and hence were sent packing. This dismissive attitude ignited an eruption of anger in Jesus (Mark 10:13–14). Yet some things don't change. Two commentators, writing in the context of two-thirds world development, express concern about how children are often ignored or misused in development strategy.

"It is odd that parent's treatment of children is not a matter of massive global public concern, analysis, critical learning and sharing." – Robert Chambers[158]

"We deem children highly in emotional terms but deem them 'useless' in any formal sense, excluding their contributions from measurements of work and

production, and making them invisible in statistics, debate and policy making." – *Michael Edwards*[159]

**Jesus in contrast, far from seeing children as 'useless' conferred VIP status upon them.**

- To RECEIVE A child is to receive Jesus (Mark 9:37)
- THEY ARE MODELS of how to 'receive the kingdom' (Mark 10:14,15)
- CHILDREN ARE TO be nurtured both in community and home (Deut 6,11)
- THEY ARE CALLED to worship (Psalm 8:2). Praise is not something they will learn to bring when they are older – it is their role now. Children give praise to Jesus even when adults reject him (Matt 21:15)
- CHILDREN ARE AGENTS of God's mission. Children are not only the ones who follow, but the ones whom God sends to lead (Isaiah 11:6). God chooses children as key figures in the biblical narrative: Isaac, Moses, Samuel and David.
- THEY ARE UNCONDITIONALLY loved. Jesus has simply a blessing for children brought to him: he made no demands, offered them no challenges, and didn't even tell them a story with a spiritual point (Matt 19:13–15)
- CHILDREN ARE A key focus in the ministry of Christ. Jesus heals children (Luke 7, 8) and welcomes them (Mark 10); he uses children as examples of humility (Luke 18:17); he warns of judgement for those who harm children (Matt 18:5–6, 10) and he highly values them (Matt 18:12–14).

"**New Testament worship seemed to have involved all generations. Children were taken for granted as part of the church. Modern theological debates about baptism have tended to obscure the sociological fact that the whole structure of the early church was family based. If a child belonged in a family, then he or she belonged to the church. This is never spelled out categorically simply because it was taken for granted.**" – *John Drane*[160]

**How can we ensure that the catholicity of the gospel continues to include and value children?**

**We must:**

- RECOGNIZE THAT A better future begins with 'better' children; most life-shaping decisions, including faith decisions, are made before the age of eighteen.
- SEE CHILDREN AS fellow disciples, and value and celebrate their spirituality rather than marginalising and dismissing it as 'only a childhood decision'.
- INVEST KEY RESOURCES into the lives of children. How do their facilities in the local church compare with those that the adults enjoy?

> **Whatever beliefs a person embraces when they are young are unlikely to change as they age.**

- REFUSE TO RELEGATE them to 'the church of tomorrow' and recognise that they are fully fledged members of the household of faith now.
- CELEBRATE THEIR INSIGHTS as children, and learn from their simplicity and faith.
- ACKNOWLEDGE THAT THE healthy transformation of a community is always confirmed by valuing children. In desperate situations of poverty, a child's needs are often sacrificed for the well-being of parents. Contrarily, a healthy community invests in its children.

Margaret Withers, Archbishop's Officer for Evangelism among Children for the Church of England, writes:

"**Underriver, a village in Kent, had no children at the church until it started a series of Saturday**

activity days. These have led to a monthly family service with up to 70 people attending it.

'Messy Church' in Cowplain near Portsmouth is a group of parents and children meeting after school for craft activities and worship, followed by a high tea. Kids Klubs and Cell Groups, usually in areas of deprivation, attract children who have no previous link with any church. Some inevitably drop out, but many stay and some make a Christian commitment, usually baptism.

In Great Dunmow, Essex, new toddler group 'Squeals on Wheels' has given young parents and their children a chance to play and pray together, and the congregation has gained a sense of mission and hope for the future through it.

Three things characterise these children's groups.

Not one of the churches has a large congregation or is well resourced. Some of them are tiny and struggling and the cost of most of these projects was minimal.

They were usually the result of one or two people recognising a need in the community and stimulating others to support it.

Most significantly, most activities have changed the whole congregation. It may have grown in numbers; the development may have led to something else; it has been given a new sense of hope and vitality by the presence of children – or all three! As children's worship and activities are becoming widespread, the inevitable question is 'what of the future?' One thing is certain. While churches wait for children to come to them and confine their ministries to Sunday, numbers will continue to dwindle. We need to resource and celebrate these children's acts of worship and activities as genuine ways of worshipping God and hearing the gospel message. They offer many opportunities and we must be prepared for changes and surprises along the way.

The potential growth from this work is enormous. Clergy and children's leaders are hungry for help and need the recognition and means to develop their ministries. This includes accessible training and resources to equip them for the task. The real battle for children being part of the church is not, however, just about equipping workers to lead children's groups or training clergy in a ministry among children, important though they are. *It is about recognising children as fellow disciples wherever they are, and changing the hearts and minds of adult Christians so that they can share responsibility for the church's mission among the youngest and most vulnerable generation.* – *Margaret Withers*[161] *(italics added)*

Children are more open and receptive to the gospel than at any other time in their lives.

"The data shows that churches can have a very significant impact on the worldview of people, but they must start with an intentional process introduced to people at a very young age. Waiting until someone is in their teens or young adult years misses the window of opportunity." – *George Barna*[162]

Barna concluded from his research in the United States[163] that:

- BETWEEN THE AGES of five and twelve, lifelong habits, values, beliefs and attitudes are formed. Whatever beliefs a person embraces when they are young are unlikely to change as the individual ages.
- IF A PERSON does not embrace Jesus Christ as Saviour before they reach their teenage years, they most likely never will, although university years are often another season of openness and questioning.

Barna's conclusions could imply that children should be targeted as likely prospects so that they will be committed Christians in later life, rather than taking the vital and relevant message of the gospel to them where they are now in their lives.

Children live in many and varied circumstances, yet they face remarkably similar realities across the world.

- HUNGER FOR SIGNIFICANT relationships.
- DISAPPEARING CHILDHOOD THROUGH exposure to adult lifestyles and expectations at ever-earlier ages.
- RAPID CHANGE, ESPECIALLY in technology, where children's understanding often outstrips that of their parents.
- MEDIA INFLUENCE, INCLUDING the promotion of celebrities as negative role models.
- PEER PRESSURE.
- UNPREDICTABILITY RANGING FROM global uncertainty to fragile family situations.

> **The society that neglects its children is one generation away from destruction.**

- EROSION OF BELIEFS as modern thought challenges traditional or religious values, and the church fails to equip children for Monday morning life.

**A child needs the gospel to equip them for the rigours of being a child in today's world.**

❝…there must be for Christians a particular focus of concern for children; and not merely the children of their own household, nor just the children of the church community, but children simply as children, wherever they are and in whatever need they find themselves.❞
– *William Strange*[164]

❝May we enlarge our vision for relevance of the gospel to the millions of children… They need the love of Christ

every bit as much as the rest of us and the evangelistic task is urgent.❞
– *Francis Bridger*[165]

In some Western countries, up to 50 per cent of the nation's churches don't have children's ministry. In England, two of every five churches have no children attending.[166] **If we are to effectively serve our children and invite them to know Christ, there are some barriers to overcome.**

- WE MUST REJECT a fear that all evangelism among children is manipulative, but also
- WE MUST TOTALLY avoid 'evangelism' that is manipulative, lest children be inappropriately pressured into faith, and their openness and receptivity abused.
- WE MUST REJECT the attitude that values children's evangelism as a 'bait' to reach parents rather than as a legitimate activity in its own right.
- WE MUST NOT make an artificial distinction between evangelism and discipleship. This implies that the evangelist's responsibility is complete when the child's first response is made.

❝The society that neglects its children is one generation away from destruction.❞
– *Margaret Mead*[167]

**Jesus' catholicity meant that those previously excluded were now honoured guests.**

# 4 ONE PEOPLE: IN THE LIFE OF JESUS

## So what? Person to Person: For individual reflection

"Joy is the serious business of heaven."     – C.S. Lewis

**As you read this passage from John Ortberg think how children reflect God.**

I was trying to get one of my children Mallory dried off after having her bath. She was doing the Dee Dah Day dance, which consisted of her running around in circles, singing over and over again Dee Dah Day, Dee Dah Day. It is a relatively simple dance expressing great joy. When she is too happy to hold it in any longer, when words are inadequate to give voice to her euphoria, she has to dance to release her joy. So she does the Dee Dah Day.

On this particular occasion, I was irritated. "Mallory, Hurry!" I prodded. So she did – she began running in circles faster and faster and chanting "Dee dah day" more rapidly. "No Mallory, that's not what I mean! Stop with the dee dah day stuff, and get over here so I can dry you off. Hurry!"

Then she asked a profound question: "Why?"

I had no answer. I had nowhere to go, nothing to do, no meeting to attend, no sermons to write. I was just so used to hurrying, so preoccupied with my own little agenda, so trapped in this rut of moving from one task to another, that here was life, here was joy, here was an invitation to the dance right in front of me – and I was missing it. So I got up, and Mallory and I did the Dee Dah Day dance together.

Reflecting on this afterward, I realised that most of my life is spent in transit: trying to get somewhere, waiting to begin, driving some place, standing in line, waiting for a meeting to end, trying to get a task completed, worrying about something bad that might happen, or being angry about something that did happen. These are all moments when I am not likely to be fully present, not to be aware of the voice and purpose of God. I am impatient. I am, almost literally, killing time. Ironically, often the thing that keeps me from experiencing joy is my preoccupation with self. It keeps me from noticing and delighting in the myriad small gifts God offers each day.

Life is not that way for Mallory. Her self is unstuffed. She just lives. Life is a series of dee dah day moments. Not every moment of life is happy, of course. There are still occasions that call for tears – skinned knees, lost friends. But each moment is pregnant with possibility. Mallory doesn't miss many of them. She is teaching me about joy. And I need to learn. Joy is at the heart of God's plan for human beings.

Jesus came as the Joy-bringer. The joy we see in the happiest child is but a fraction of the joy that resides in the heart of God.

– John Ortberg, from his book *The Life you've Always Wanted*

**As church and individuals we often don't stop and appreciate the joy children carry or allow them to influence and inspire us.**

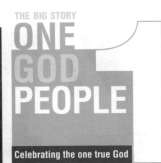

## So what? People to People: For group discussion together

### Single parents who have never been married – a stigmatised group in our day?

Consider this letter from Jenny Clarke (*reproduced with her permission*).

Dear Jeff,

I'm asking you to consider helping me and others like me.

You see, the problem is that becoming a parent drew me back into the church after a long layoff but it has also been the factor that is now pushing me away from the church. The reason for this is that I am a single mother – not a divorcee, not a widow, not separated, but I became pregnant outside of wedlock and I am no longer with the father of my child.

The church has an attitude to single mothers like me that continues to label us. Sure, I made a big mistake ten years ago that I deeply regret (not the outcome though – my beautiful child is one of God's greatest gifts to me) but with God's grace I am changed. Unfortunately the church does not allow for this.

Single mothers like me are constantly held up as fearful sinners. Some examples:

I sat next to a loud, God-fearing man in house group who announced that all sinners should be welcomed into the church and then went on to list the types he meant: wife beaters, drug pushers, murderers and single mothers.... I was too stunned to do what I should have done, like encourage him to wear his coffee...

Another time I was helping to organise the catering for the wedding of a dear friend's daughter in our church – my friend didn't have a lot of money so I organised a group of friends to provide the food at cost. The night before the wedding she was trying to work out the order of play for the reception. She turned to me for advice and I told her that as I had never been married I really didn't have a clue. Shocked and flustered (she must have assumed I was divorced) she said, 'Oh don't worry about

me, I've seen it all – drug pushers – the lot'. That certainly took the shine off my good deed....

Thinking that maybe it was just my church that had an issue with this, I signed up for single parent's week in the hope of finding some acceptance and understanding. The leaders were married – not a good start! During the opening address the speaker said we were all there for different reasons, we were either divorced, separated, widowed or well, you know.... I felt like leaping to my feet to shout loudly 'Yes I had sex outside marriage and yes I got pregnant and yes I took the tough route and didn't have an abortion!!!' It still was a fabulous week but I didn't find the acceptance I longed for.

After all, where am I so different to anyone else? How many Christians really were virgins when they married? How many of the thousands of Christians in this country secretly had abortions when they got it wrong?

The church will take a long time to really embrace people like me. There will always be people who casually write me and my like off as terrible sinners with a label.

Maybe one day the thousands of unmarried mothers out there can find a place in their local church where they can find the peace, love and acceptance that Jesus promised all of us.

I am proud of my beautiful nine-year-old son, and just want to find a way that unmarried mothers like me can really feel accepted and supported in our daily effort to bring our children up as Christians.

With lots of hope and lots more thanks

Jenny Clarke (Miss)

• How does Jenny's letter make you feel?

• Is the situation she describes an accurate summary of the way things might be in your church?

• What steps can we take to resolve the hurt that she describes?

# The Message of the Kingdom: it's Sunday, but Monday's Coming

The lifestyle and practice of Jesus showed that God reaches out to all. **His message, the news of the kingdom, shows that this message is for all of life.**

❝The kingdom of God is not a theological phrase, but is now a name with a human face.❞ — *Lesslie Newbigin*

❝Jesus is the kingdom of God taking sandals and walking.❞ — *E. Stanley Jones*

### The main thing: the kingdom

❝Jesus went throughout Galilee, teaching in their synagogues, preaching the good news of the kingdom, and healing every disease and sickness among the people.❞ — *Matthew 4:23*

**The theme of the kingdom of God (Matthew uses the term 'kingdom of heaven') was the main message of Jesus.** Tragically, we too often think of the kingdom as being somewhere people go to after death. Though this is true, it is only then that we will know the *fullness* of the kingdom – life absolutely under the reign and rule of God – the kingdom is also here, among us now, as God's order is established in the earth, and as lives and decisions are submitted to his will. Michael Green says the kingdom was 'Jesus' prime concern'.

- MATTHEW USES THE term kingdom of heaven 32 times.

- MARK OPENS HIS Gospel with Isaiah's and John's voices announcing the one to come, and then Jesus arrives and announces – 'the kingdom of God is near!' (Mark 1:15)
- THE KINGDOM WAS the subject of Jesus' first sermon (Mark 1:14), and was the only thing he called the gospel. (Matt 4:23)
- THE PARABLES OF Jesus were mostly 'windows' to shed light on what the kingdom is like.
- JESUS TAUGHT THAT understanding the kingdom was the key to understanding his teaching (Luke 8:10), that the kingdom should be the very first thing we seek (Matt 6:33) and calls us to pray for the kingdom to come (Matt 6:10).
- THE KINGDOM WAS the focus of his teaching to the disciples during his last forty days on earth (Acts 1:3).
- THE STORY OF the first church closes with the news that 'Boldly and without hindrance he [Paul] preached the kingdom of God and taught about the Lord Jesus Christ' (Acts 28:31); Jesus taught that the kingdom 'will be preached in the whole world as a testimony to all nations, and then the end will come' (Matt 24:14).

❝I cannot help wondering out loud why I haven't heard more about the kingdom in the thirty years I have been a Christian. I certainly read about it enough in the Bible… but I honestly cannot remember any pastor whose ministry I have been under actually preaching a sermon on the kingdom of God. As I rummage through my own sermon barrel, I now realize that I

myself have never preached a sermon on it. Where has the kingdom been?"
*– C. Peter Wagner*

"During the past sixteen years I can recollect only two occasions on which I have heard sermons specifically devoted to the theme of the kingdom of God…. I find this silence rather surprising because it is universally agreed by New Testament scholars that the central theme of the teaching of Jesus was the kingdom of God."
*– I. Howard Marshall*

**The kingdom must feature more centrally in our thinking.**

**But what exactly is this kingdom of God?**

**At the time of Jesus, the Jews were looking for 'the kingdom of God' – to them it was not a woolly existence after death, but a down to earth political state of affairs where Israel, a nation occupied by Rome, would be free to enjoy her own land with God as king.**

"The kingdom of God was simply a Jewish way of talking about Israel's God becoming King." *– Tom Wright*[168]

As we've seen in our look at the people of God in the Old Testament, the plan had always been that God alone would be king over his people, but from the 11th century BC, when sometimes-good-but-mostly-bad King Saul reigned, with the exception of the reigns of David and Solomon the concept of kingship went downhill. And even the brilliance of David's reign was seen as a foretaste of something even far better to come. From David's family line would come a great king who would build a kingdom that would last forever.

**In Jesus' time, there was disagreement about how this new kingdom would come. At least four ideas were popular.**

- THE SADDUCEES, THE ruling group of priests who held most of the power, taught that maintaining the status

quo with continued sacrificial worship in the temple would usher in the time of God's reign.

- THE ESSENES, WHO hated the temple because it had been built by King Herod the Great, withdrew to a separated community just 15 miles or so from Jerusalem, by the shore of the Dead Sea – where the Dead Sea scrolls were later found.

- THE PHARISEES INSISTED, as we've seen, that withdrawal from everyday life was not necessary, but a revival of ceremonial and everyday holiness would prompt God to intervene on beleaguered Israel's behalf.

- THE ZEALOTS, A clandestine resistance force, took matters into their own hands and instigated uprisings to try to overthrow the hated occupiers.

**Then Jesus came. Little wonder that there was such a stir when he announced the kingdom was coming and was here.** And he used more than words to let everyone know the epic news.

- JESUS RODE INTO Jerusalem on a donkey, just as Zechariah had prophesied Israel's king would ride into the city on a colt (Zech 9:9). The symbolism was obvious.

"No one in their right mind would enter the city this way – it would be like hiring a presidential limousine to enter Washington, which is pretty crazy, unless, of course, you are the president." *– Graham Tomlin*[169]

- HE ANNOUNCED JUDGEMENT to Israel in the cursing of the fig tree (as we've already seen, a symbol of Israel).

- HE CLEARED THE temple and announced its soon demise – the brief act that, according to most scholars, finally triggered his arrest and eventual execution.[170] As the temple stood for Israel's survival, this was a radical and stark act, but not an anti-Semitic one; his actions were obviously taken out of love for the nation and for his father. Only David's promised king could rebuild the temple (2 Sam 7:13) – and now a completely new temple, not built with hands, and not actually a temple but a kingdom without ethnic or geographical boundaries,

was being established (John 18:36). The king was taking his throne back.

Now the opportunity had arrived to live as those who place every area of their lives under his loving reign.

## The kingdom reminds us again of the corporate

The concept of a kingdom speaks to us of a corporate entity – a king or queen rules over a collective people. So the truth of the kingdom is fundamentally social; speaking not only about the relationship between citizen and ruler, but about relationships between citizens and relationships among kingdoms. It is more than a spiritual condition.

"The kingdom is something that people enter, not something that enters them. It is a state of affairs, not just a state of mind."
— *Allen Verhey*[171]

But just as some individuals are of course able to make choices about what earthly kingdom they will reside in, so we can make choices about our allegiance and residency under God's rule – or otherwise.

## The kingdom and the church are not the same

**The kingdom – the reign of God – obviously existed before the church, and will continue throughout eternity when the entity of the church will have discontinued its earthly existence. The kingdom represents the rule of Christ over all peoples, principalities and powers.**

The distinction between church and kingdom is vital – when we see that the church, and the structures and programmes that the church creates, are *servants* of the kingdom and not the kingdom itself, then we are able to remain both humble and be open to change. This also prompts us to realize that God's activity and beauty are not limited to the church. **He is the Creator!**

So we can admire and give thanks for wonderful art and musical genius, whether it comes from 'the church'

– Christian artists or composers – or not. Love, kindness, generosity, wisdom and understanding are not limited to the confines of the church: beauty is found everywhere, because the influence and reign of God is found in the most unexpected places.

"The distinction between church and kingdom is very, very important. It keeps the church humble and understated, and is a healthy corrective to the triumphalism that so easily creeps into any institution that believes that in some way it has a special role to play in God's plans."
— *Graham Tomlin*[172]

## The kingdom calls for total allegiance

"All too often in Western society, people respond to the message of the evangelist by adding a new compartment to their life."
— *Roy McCloughry*[173]

**To step into the kingdom is to surrender to Christ every right, rather than 'getting a little religion' like adding an extension to a house. This is how life is supposed to be for every human being on earth – living under the reign and order of the King in his kingdom. The language of rebirth that John's Gospel gives us (John 3) is completely compatible with the language of the Synoptic Gospels (Matthew, Mark and Luke). John's understanding of spiritual transformation and the language of the rule of God are two sides of the same coin.**

For the earliest Christians, this call to total allegiance meant they had to acknowledge that Herod the Great was not king of the Jews, as he prided himself, and Caesar was not lord. Suffering is expected for those who profess loyalty to Christ, including ridicule, outright hostility and persecution, as we will see later today.

**It is interesting that the leading contender for our loyalty is money; Jesus specifically pointed to 'mammon' as the top candidate for misguided worship (Matt 6:24).**

## The kingdom is surprising

Jesus' entry into Jerusalem was both a fulfilment and a surprise. Other Messianic figures offered aggressive and militaristic solutions to Israel's immense problems, but Jesus came riding on a colt – a symbol of peace, of a life without chariots and war-horses (Zech 9:10) – announcing peace to the Gentiles. He is the king of the Jews, crowned on a cross not a throne. His is the kingdom where a radical set of values reign – and to be a citizen of that kingdom means learning that new, radical way of life.

"Again and again in parable, sermon and act, Jesus startles us. Good guys turn out to be bad guys. Those we expect to receive the reward get a spanking instead. Those who think they are headed for heaven land in hell. Things are reversed. Paradox, irony and surprise permeate the teachings of Jesus. The least are the greatest. The immoral receive forgiveness and blessing. Adults become like children. The religious miss the heavenly banquet. The pious receive curses. We're baffled and perplexed. Should we laugh or should we cry?"
– *Donald Kraybill*[174]

## The kingdom is about actions, not just theories or ideologies

Jesus didn't come just to add some fascinating theological titbits to the religious smorgasbord of his day, but to put a new entity into place in the bringing of the kingdom. That's not to say that words and truths are not absolutely vital – nevertheless, the kingdom is about actions and words.

"It's sometimes said that the heart of Jesus' ministry lay in his teaching, and that his actions (for example, his miracles and acted parables) were secondary, almost a distraction from his teaching. Actually, the reverse is true. Jesus came primarily not to teach some new ideas, but to bring in the kingdom of God. His words are in fact a commentary on his actions. They explain the significance of what is taking place as he heals the sick, raises the dead, walks on water, confronts the temple and goes to his death."
– *Graham Tomlin*[175]

Lesslie Newbigin[176] identifies the pattern of event/explanation in the Gospels. In the long series of teaching material in John, most of the teaching is an explanation of something Jesus has done: healing the paralytic, feeding the multitude, giving sight to the blind man, raising a dead body to life. We'll return to this thought tomorrow when we think about mission.

## The kingdom is a party

"Wherever Jesus went there seemed to be a celebration; the tradition of festive meals, at which Jesus welcomed all and sundry, is one of the most securely established features of almost all recent scholarly portraits. He was… making these meals and their free-for-all welcome a central feature of his programme."
– *Tom Wright*[177]

The living, active church is called to be the primary sign of the kingdom – a living banquet, a working model of life lived under the love and lordship of Jesus, but a party with an open-door policy where all are invited to come in from the cold and join in with the fun. Graham Tomlin uses the analogy of the church being like the 12th century character of legend Robin Hood.

In that story, the honourable and good King Richard is absent from the country, and so the land is ruled by his despicable brother, King John. Harsh taxation and national oppression lead Robin, Maid Marion and a band of 'merry men' to go underground – specifically into the undergrowth – in Sherwood Forest. Their acts of defiance and charity (robbing the rich to give to the poor) keep the knowledge of the good-king-to-come alive. And they are a mischievous, subversive lot, characterized by their playful ability to laugh in the face of suffering, because they know that the reign of evil is but temporary. As we delight in story, laughter, outrageous celebration and kindness, we become living signs of a reign that is here but is yet to come in its fullness.

"The images Jesus used to describe the kingdom were always full of delight. It is like a feast with lavish food

and great hilarity, or a woman finding a priceless lost necklace and throwing a party to celebrate. The picture of a bunch of outlaws celebrating with huge joyful meals deep in the forest in defiance of the false powers is the same kind of story. This is no stern, solemn king, exercising a humourless, cold, rule. It is the rule of the gracious host, inviting us into his home, the place where he is in charge, and where there is lots of deep, rich laughter. **Miserable, gloomy and dull churches have simply missed the point.**" – *Graham Tomlin*[178]

## The kingdom: it's Sunday, but Monday's coming

Because the truth of the kingdom calls us to live all of life under God, and for God, the teaching of the church must equip us for every day of life – for Mondays as well as Sundays.

> **The church has got to be a place where the world and people's concerns about it are taken seriously and addressed. It is no good preaching week in, week out, about speaking in tongues, sanctification, or how to praise the Lord with the latest Spring Harvest tape, if we aren't also preaching about how to be Christians at work, what God thinks and feels about the world we live in, and what kind of politics honours the King of kings.**" – *Simon Jones*[179]

We can tell what's important to a church (or any organization) by the heroes it celebrates and the stories it tells, Mark Greene says. Are most of the church's heroes, preachers and teachers white, and mainly male?

> **Why are you a hero if you teach a Sunday school, but not if you teach 150 Muslim, Hindu and secular kids in an inner-city school Monday through Friday.**" – *Mark Greene*[180]

Consider the experience of Brookside Church in Reading. They decided to change the format of their quarterly church business meeting to focus on what was happening *beyond* the building, rather than *inside* it. It was to be a 'business

of the people of the church' meeting. They held a kind of market in the church hall – with estate agents, policemen and policewomen, a physiotherapist with a dummy and school teachers all available to talk about what they did most of their lives. At the end of the evening, there was a time of prayer for all.

The next quarter the focus was on what people did in leisure time. School governors, members of football teams, Girl Guides and Boy Scout leaders all were saying, This is what we do. They knew they were valued. The church was hugely encouraged as they saw the scale of their influence severally and together; more than this, they were really valuing what they said they valued.

## So what? Person to Person: For individual reflection

Many of us gladly embraced the rule and reign of Jesus years ago. Reflect on these words: Do thoughts here connect with where you are right now?

### Waterside[181]

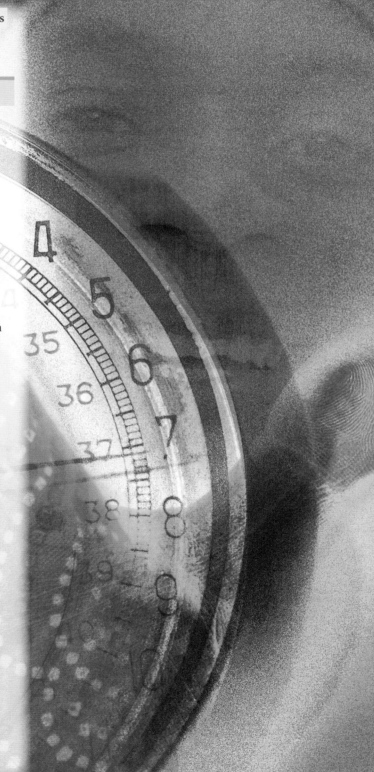

I used to skip and play
Beside still, clean waters
Diamonds sparkling, scattered by the sun
Dancing above the surface
Pure, holy cold blue
Baptizing me in laughter

But there are days when still has turned to stale
Technicolor turned black and white, a tiresome tale
My visibility reduced to just an inch
The see-through stream, now muddied
With pains and stains of what I could or should have been

My pool at times a grimy puddle
A septic tank for others trash, and mine too
Those discarded, putrid sacks
Cluttering my hope, I fight for air

I'm scared.

Fill me, Holy Spirit, now
Gush, rush all through me
I may not jump to dizzy heights
Or go on flights of fancy
Or soar on supernatural thermals
So that some will reach out now and touch their tv screen
And I'll been seen
As someone, really someone
But take me once again to that cold blue
And there with you I'll stay
And play awhile
And there, together, on that warm bank
We'll love and laugh and nap and dash
And splash others with your love.

## So what? People to People: For group discussion together

Do our churches take seriously the call to empower and equip people as priests, prophets and politicians in the workplace and wider world? Is there adequate teaching, prayer focus and space given to help us understand each other's worlds? How well does our Sunday morning connect with Monday morning?

"The key problem is not that we have failed to notice that work is significant, but rather that we have not noticed that all of life is significant to the creator and redeemer God."
– *Mark Greene*[182]

One way to help connect Sunday morning with Monday morning is to have a 3T (this time tomorrow) spot in each Sunday morning service (perhaps before a time of prayer) when a member of the congregation shares what they will be doing on Monday morning.

Could this idea be incorporated into the life of the church that you attend?

For more resources visit www.worknetuk.org

## Teaching Block 3:

# One catholic church in a fragmented world

**Christ is creating a universal family of all peoples, where his rule and reign are established in every area of our lives: one people, under God. But is that a romantic notion, or a reality?**

❝The Lord's people, if they are to be faithful and reflective of our King, must have global eyes and global hearts. Our destiny is bound up with the global church. And in our lifetime, the church has become global as never before. It is Christians of all people who should have a deep sense of connection with people everywhere, and especially with brothers and sisters in Christ. As such, we need new glasses to see what God is doing in his world in our day. Global eyesight, and global hearts.❞
– *Rose Dowsett*[183]

Even though we are not (at the time of writing) in outright world war, the tragic fact remains that dividing lines between cultures and nations are becoming more distinct – and dangerous. The church faces the huge challenge of not only *speaking* the gospel of reconciliation into the cauldron of hostility, but also of *modelling* the reality that nationhood and ethnicity are secondary markers of identity.

In Christ, we can experience a oneness that transcends tribal affiliations. This is also true when we consider divisions between generations. Can we, the church, be an example of young and old and everything in between being together, with mutual respect and honour, in a society that is fragmented by age and fashion?

Our Christian witness and mission will lack plausibility unless we are able to demonstrate practical cooperation and unity. Spring Harvest is an example of ecumenism, with many people from different traditions coming together to learn and worship. **Can we be a catholic, universal family? To move further towards this catholicity, we must have listening ears, joined hands and shared tears.**

### Listening ears

Understanding the catholic nature of the church helps us avoid the common fallacy that Christianity is a Western religion, an idea that quickly leads Westerners to the false notion that they are the 'enlightened educators'. The human quest for God is obviously not limited to Europe. Western explorers and missionaries often claimed that Africans, for example, had no religion and were uneducated, simplistic and shamefully ignorant. But Christianity on that continent pre-dates Western mission and has its roots in the Day of Pentecost.

In 1960, more than 70 per cent of the church was Western, but indigenous mission movements were beginning to emerge out of indigenous churches. Since the 1980s the non-Western church has grown at such a rate that the global church is now more than 70 per cent non-Western. The UK church is now part of the minority.

"Danger comes when we are unable to accept the limitations of our understanding, and attempt to formulate systems which cannot tolerate gaps or humble recognition of our inadequacies. Evangelicals are often unable to distinguish between the sufficiency of Scripture and the exhaustiveness of Scripture, between divine inspiration and human fallibility in interpretation. More than we know, we have absorbed the Enlightenment heresy that man can master the universe, and have applied that to the theological enterprise as well. Having formulated our faith to our satisfaction, we do not like to listen carefully to our brothers and sisters in other parts of the world who have read the same Word, but from a different context, and who then 'arrange the data' differently. It is absolutely true that there is no meaningful unity, no unity that flows from the Spirit, that is not unity rooted in God's truth. But God, who speaks Chinese and Arabic and Swahili quite as fluently as he speaks English, may have many gentle corrections to work in us as our brothers and sisters respond to his Word and tell of what they hear and see. It is part of our contemporary family privilege and family responsibility to respect, enjoy, and fellowship with our siblings. In each other's company, we have the marvellous opportunity to grasp more deeply and richly the nuances of God's Word."   – Rose Dowsett[184]

**And we must be careful lest we think that God is most at work wherever *we* are, in the so-called 'important' centres of commerce and industry in the West. The planet-saving ministry of Jesus was mostly expressed in the backwater that was Galilee, on the edge of Israel.**

Kosuke Koyama reminds us that since Jesus is the true centre of the kingdom of God, where *he* is becomes the centre.[185] The power players of Jerusalem were forced to go to the humblest villages to see their adversary in action, so the location that seemed to be on the periphery was actually the epicentre of God's activity. The obscure is far from God-forsaken. On the contrary, when we posture ourselves in this stance of humility we are able to sit at the feet of our brothers and sisters from the worldwide family and learn from their differing and vital perspectives.

"Latin Americans such as Rene Padilla and Samuel Escobar brought such ground-breaking papers to the epochal Lausanne Congress on World Evangelization in 1974, contributing significantly to the Manifesto, and helping restore to much of world evangelicalism a grasp of the holistic nature of the gospel. This had been very much a part of our evangelical heritage, but had been eclipsed in the rise of late nineteenth and early twentieth century liberalism. It needed our non-Western brothers and sisters to bring us back on course."   – Rose Dowsett[186]

Other vital insights from non-Western theologians have helped us in our understanding of:

- THE NATURE of the spirit world
- PHYSICAL HEALING AND the atonement
- MISSIONAL CHURCH IN cultures dominated by other faiths
- REVELATION BEING FOUND in pre- and non-Christian communities.

**Our wider family may help us to reconsider our entire approach to theology.** Rose Dowsett again:

"We tend to identify serious theology with closely-reasoned, linear-thinking prose. That's the way it has been done for centuries in the West, so we assume that it must be the best way to do it. Yet most of the world's people are not analytical, linear thinkers, and in fact fewer and fewer Britons are. As it happens, most of the Bible is not written in this vein, either. So, while many in the Reformed tradition see Romans as the pinnacle of biblical revelation, and teach the rest of Scripture through its particular theological grid, many of our Majority World friends are much more comfortable with the narratives of the Old Testament and of the Gospels, with the parables, and with the proverbs. In the final analysis, we all need all of it: the whole Word.

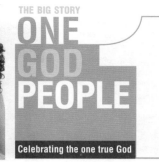

Yet the genres which most readily resonate with our own particular context will often provide a key for how we formulate our theology most meaningfully and transmit it most effectively. John and Charles Wesley taught theology by putting content full words to catchy melodies, shamelessly hijacking pub tunes among others. Why? Because they were memorable and already familiar, and the illiterate along with the educated could internalise precious truths. Graham Kendrick and others do the same in our generation, making theology accessible and mind-shaping to many. In different parts of the world evangelical family, theology may be transmitted through storytelling or celebration, hymns and ballads, genealogies and dramatic parables."
– *Rose Dowsett*[187]

**We have a vast family to listen to and learn from.**

## Hands joined

'Ethnic' and 'black majority' churches have become a familiar phenomenon in the UK in the last twenty years, especially in the more multicultural population centres like London.

Mark Sturge, a former director of the African and Caribbean Evangelical Alliance (www.acea-uk.org), classifies this movement into five broad groups.

- CHURCHES FROM THE African Caribbean diaspora
- CHURCHES FROM THE African diaspora
- BLACK CHURCHES WITHIN historic denominations
- BLACK CHURCHES WITHIN white (Pentecostal) denominations
- AFRICAN AND CARIBBEAN spiritual churches.

Many urban black churches have over 1,000 members, while *KICC*, *Jesus House*, *Ruach Ministries*, *Glory House*, *New Wine* and *Calvary Baptist Church* have between two and ten thousand members; Peter Brierley's research indicates that 51 per cent of church attendance in London consists of black and ethnic Christians.

Much of this growth is not because of necessity created by marginalisation, segregation or prejudice, but because of passionate missionary endeavour.

"I just don't like the terminology Black Majority Church! And I would like to go on record stating that certain myths need to be laid to rest! Many, if not most of these ethnic churches were not birthed out of segregation, marginalisation or discrimination. Yes, we will not discount totally some of these factors, but the major Caribbean denominations evolved out of denominational expansion and missionary zeal. A lot of these churches like *The Church of God in Christ* emerged out of house fellowships around 1951. They blossomed as outgrowths of established churches in the Caribbean and merely continued their faith, liturgy and worship as practised back home." – *Bishop Joe Aldred, Secretary for Minority Ethic Affairs Churches Together in England*[188]

The not-so-positive news is that often the interface between white and black churches is intermittent, as each tends to support their own initiatives and conferences. The hard question must be asked: does this situation of congregations organised around ethnicity truly reflect the universality of the church? The situation is similar in the United States; 'mixed' churches (or 'blended' as they are tagged) are rare in America, representing only eight per cent of the churchgoing population. Researchers regard a 'mixed' congregation as one with at least twenty per cent of its members providing racial or ethnic diversity.

"The church, which is meant to be an example, a proof of the way in which division and faction and conflict and suspicion can be overcome, has far too frequently fragmented along lines of doctrine, geography, race, language, class, age and taste. ... One church I worked for has a Ghanaian fellowship that meets in its building on Sunday afternoons, separately from the mainly white, mainly young, mainly urban professionals that meet there on Sunday evenings. There are many reasons for such practice, and I'm not blaming anyone for it; it is easier to associate with people of similar background and tradition. I am simply pointing out that it fails to demonstrate the achievement of the Cross."

– *Michael Lloyd*[189]

"If our churches are still divided in any way along racial or cultural lines, Paul would have to say that our gospel, our very grasp of the meaning of Jesus' death, is called into question."

– *Tom Wright*[190]

"11AM on Sunday is the most segregated hour of the week in America."

– *Martin Luther King Jnr.*

The poorest record on diversity, with only two to three per cent mixed on average, belongs to historic Protestant churches, which ironically were among the first to proclaim the ideal of integrated congregations.

As we consider this challenge, the issue is obviously not to call the existence of ethnic churches into question, as if they do not have the right to exist and 'white' congregations do, but rather to ask questions about the reasons they need to exist. **If we assume that ethnic congregations are not ideal because they mirror fragmentation, but are necessary because of the marginalisation, special challenges and threat to ethnic identity and customs that exist among ethnicities – and in order that their missionary efforts will be most effective – then we must surely work towards greater mutual cooperation, respect, co-celebration, rejoicing in diversity, learning, prayer, and the sharing of resources. But there will be challenges to fulfilment of this vision.**

## Different understandings of the local church

There are two basic understandings of what it means to be 'church' – the 'parish' model and the 'gathered' model. The former undergirds Anglican and Catholic churches, and of course many non-conformist churches operate on a locality model, where there is a sense of pastoral responsibility towards the local community, which in turn may have a sense of ownership towards its parish or local church.

The gathered church is more natural to non-indigenous and non-traditional church groups. Its emphasis is more on doing church, meeting as a gathered community from far and near. Many people will travel miles to be part of the fellowship, and might have no particular contact with the community in which the church building is placed. This can lead to a lack of commitment to the surrounding community, and a lack of attention to the work of the Spirit in that locality.

## Different attitudes to mission

Compare these two mission statements.

From a black majority leader – mission is:

- EXALTING AND HONOURING the name of God
- THE PHYSICAL PRESENCE of a strong and vibrant worshipping community
- PREACHING AND TEACHING the Word of God
- OFFERING THE EUCHARIST
- BAPTISING OF BELIEVERS
- ACCEPTANCE OF BELIEVERS into fellowship.

The 'five marks of mission' – originally set out by the Lambeth Anglican Conference in 1988, and now widely used ecumenically.

Mission is:

- PROCLAIMING THE GOOD news of the kingdom
- TEACHING, BAPTISING AND nurturing new believers
- RESPONDING TO HUMAN need by loving service
- TRANSFORMING UNJUST STRUCTURES of society
- STRIVING TO SAFEGUARD the integrity of creation and sustaining and renewing the life of the earth.

In practice many so-called black majority churches are deeply involved in social issues in their community, and in wider issues of peace and justice; and many mainstream churches are far from engaged in the range of issues described by the five marks of mission.

# ONE GOD PEOPLE

Celebrating the one true God

"Freedoms Ark, pastored by Rev. Nimms Obunge, has been the precursor of the Peace Alliance. This community initiative works in partnership with the Home Office, Ken Livingstone's Cabinet, the Metropolitan Police and various local councils within and beyond the capital. … The Glory House Football Academy is probably one of the best-kept secrets within East London and has a current white majority membership of 700 East End young boys and their families."

– *Jonathan Oloyede*[191]

Nonetheless, whatever our ethnicity we are not all on the same page when it comes to defining the core purpose of church, which can be a challenge to cooperation.

## Different attitudes to worship

It is obvious that attitudes to worship reflect the culture and background of the worshipper and different theologies about worship itself. Churches differ too in their attitudes to the sacred and the profane, to the relationship between the spiritual and the physical, and in different attitudes to the concept of sanctuary.

**Behind these differences, it is important to remember that many mainstream inner-city congregations have a high proportion of black people; that whilst many black majority churches have a reputation for freedom and spontaneity in their worship, a strong sense of order underpins that freedom; and that there is as great a variety of theological outlooks and styles of worship in black majority churches as in mainstream churches.**

**In the midst of all the challenges there are hopeful developments.**

## Signs of hope: resources shared

In the west of London, congregations that identify themselves as Syrian Orthodox, Bethel Korean, Mount Zion Holiness, Vineyard, Byelorussian Orthodox, Jesus Christ of Nazareth, Christ Apostolic, Pentecostal Holiness, Beulah Apostolic and Church of God of Prophecy share buildings with Anglican parish churches. Some mainstream churches

in the inner city are struggling with large and inefficient buildings maintained by small and elderly congregations. The same part of London has a large number of ethnic minority congregations, some of whom are desperate for somewhere to worship. In 1994 about 60 per cent of Church of England parishes in the four northern archdeaconries of Southwark hosted at least one, and sometimes up to three, other congregations.

This sharing has not been without difficulty and tension. There have been many complaints, unhappy relationships and misunderstandings that do no credit to the church as a whole. Some black Christians find that they are often not treated as brothers and sisters in the body of Christ – frequently because a landlord-tenant relationship has grown up. Yet a good many sharing situations continue without friction and to mutual advantage.

**Regular meetings between leaders (and not just to resolve problems), visits between congregations to each other's worship services, and bold leadership that helps congregations to change and experiment can help us find ways to join hands together in the future.**

## Signs of hope: the family gathered for prayer

On 20 February 2006 a number of Christian leaders gathered in London. They decided to call a Global Day of Prayer on Pentecost Sunday 2007 (27 May) at West Ham Football Stadium in London.

The event is being supported by charismatic Catholics, Evangelicals, Pentecostals, Anglicans, black majority churches, Baptists, Methodists and multi-ethnic church communities all over London. Congregations will pray the same prayers of thanksgiving, supplication and intercession in various styles and liturgies. Some areas – like Southwark and Newham – are planning large celebrations in local parks.

A Global Day of Prayer DVD trailer is available for use in church services. A two minute trailer is downloadable at www.londonprayer.net/globaldayofprayer

page 95

## Signs of hope: Spring Harvest

Spring Harvest Main Event has not historically represented the colourful spectrum of the family of God in Britain. In truth, people will choose what Christian events they wish to attend and many of us, whatever our background or ethnicity, freely choose to attend denominational gatherings in preference to an event like Spring Harvest. Attempts are being made to find ways to proactively encourage the development of the Spring Harvest Main Event so that it will attract broader support from the wider church family in the UK. In 2006 a meeting was held between senior members of black majority churches and members of the Spring Harvest Leadership Team. The result of this warm and hopeful discussion is that black majority leaders are attending Spring Harvest 2007 with a view to helping shape the programme and content of the 2008 event, and encouraging members of their churches and constituencies to attend.

## Make us one

Though the skins that are stretched over us
Have shades enough
To mark a path from coal to snow
In micron increments
We are one
Though the fine lines of our features
Are freehand enough
That even smiles
Are signatures of difference
We are one

Though the cultures that encode us
Are cryptic enough
To make each one of us a mystery to the other
We are one
Though the polarities that plague us
Can have power enough
To make sparks fly
Every time we come together
We are one

Though the stories that have shaped us
Are self-penned enough

To fill a library with the secrets we each hide
And though the route maps we rely on
May be rough enough
To make finding common ground
A roller coaster ride
Though the distinctives that define us
May be deep enough
To aggravate and irritate and painfully divide
And though the languages we vocalise
Are localised enough
To keep a truckload of translators tongue-tied

We are one

Many: but one
Different: but one
Awkward: but one
Reluctant: but one
Taught: to be one
Bar none
May our maker
Make us one.

*Gerard Kelly*[192]

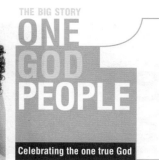

## Shared tears

"If one part suffers, every part suffers with
it."
– *1 Corinthians 12:26*

"Remember those in prison as if you were their fellow-
prisoners, and those who are ill-treated as if you
yourselves were suffering."
– *Hebrews 13:3*

"Speak up for those who cannot speak for themselves,
for the rights of all who are destitute. Speak up
and judge fairly; defend the rights of the poor and
needy."
– *Proverbs 31:8–9*

"Everyone has the right to freedom of thought, conscience and religion; this right includes freedom to
change his religion or belief, and freedom, either alone
or in community with others and in public or private,
to manifest his religion or belief in teaching, practice,
worship and observance."
– *The Universal
Declaration of Human Rights (UDHR), Article 18*

**Christians – members of our family – are being perse-
cuted on almost every continent in the world today. Their
property is being confiscated or destroyed. They are
being thrown into prison and tortured. Many are being
martyred.**

The following was contributed by Christian Solidarity
Worldwide. CSW (www.csw.org.uk) is a human rights
organisation specialising in religious freedom. CSW works
on behalf of those persecuted for their Christian beliefs and
promotes religious liberty for all.

**We must remind ourselves while reading this that there
have been too many occasions in history when the
Christian church was guilty of denying religious liberty.**

- In some expressions of Islam, people may only be
  Muslims. Some of these expressions ban polytheism,
  subjugate Jews and Christians as second-class citizens
  (*dhimmis*), and do not permit conversion out of Islam.
  Leaving Islam (apostasy) is a capital offence.

- As the church grows in Hindu and Buddhist majority
  nations, Hindu and Buddhist religious leaders who
  fear that their influence may be threatened are in the
  forefront of the persecution against the church. Citing
  religious nationalism as their justification, they claim
  Christianity will destroy national unity and identity
  which (they claim) is rooted in a common 'culture'
  (religion). The reality is that the Christians they are
  persecuting are indigenous believers from indigenous
  churches with indigenous missions and a deep desire to
  bring blessing to their nation.

- In the Indian states governed by Hindu nationalists,
  and in Buddhist Sri Lanka, religious nationalist zealots
  are calling for anti-conversion laws that would effectively
  ban Christian witness, and bar conversion to anything
  but the majority religion. Religious militants persistently
  persecute Christians. Unfortunately, many government
  officials, police and judges would rather appease the per-
  secutors than defend the rights of minority Christians.

- The situation is similar in many former Soviet states,
  where religious nationalism is being used to promote
  and justify the hegemony of politically powerful
  'traditional' religions which have a long history of coop-
  erative relationships with the ruling authorities. Russia
  expert Anneta Vyssotskaia says that the trend in some
  former Soviet states is to replace the previously all-state
  atheistic ideology with another all-state ideology,
  only this time a 'traditional' religious ideology: either
  traditional Russian Orthodox as in Russia and Belarus,
  or traditional Islam as in e.g. Uzbekistan, Kazakhstan,
  Tajikistan. Anneta says that in some small territories
  Buddhism and Judaism are considered 'traditional' and
  are therefore accepted. However, less traditional groups
  such as Protestants and Catholics are rejected and
  labelled 'sectarian' and their religious liberty is restricted.
  Traditionalists, who are usually very nationalistic,
  accuse Catholics and Protestants of attempting to divide
  the nation. Persecution is increasing. Catholics and
  Protestants are increasingly being attacked in the media

and harassed in the streets by religious nationalists, with the tacit support of the authorities.

- SOME COMMUNIST STATES, in particular Vietnam and North Korea, present a claim to religious liberty. But the reality for Christians there is very different. In China there is growing freedom for the now-flourishing registered churches that form the Three-Self Patriotic Movement – with freedom to print the Bible and meet together. However, churches that feel unable to register and to work within the legal framework can find themselves on the wrong side of the law in most painful ways. At the same time, in a nation as vast as China there may always be occasions when local authorities treat Christians in ways that are contrary to China's commitment to religious freedom. – *Peter Meadows*

- STATES THAT MAINTAIN political isolation, such as North Korea, Turkmenistan and Belarus, or states that can seduce with significant economic benefits, such as China and Saudi Arabia, persecute more severely as they are not influenced by Western advocacy. However, it is possible for a state to be open economically for the purpose of trade, capitalism and materialism, but be closed and repressing its people in terms of freedom of information, speech, association and religion, to consolidate totalitarianism.

**It must remain a moral imperative for us as *humans* to declare that human rights – the rights of *humans made in the image of God, and for whom Christ died* – take precedence over economic considerations. Furthermore, it is imperative that as *Christians* we responsibly, obediently and compassionately seek to know the truth about the persecution of our brothers and sisters in Christ who, without a media voice, suffer behind walls of propaganda.**

We must:

- COMMIT TO PRAY for the persecuted church. This is the first thing persecuted Christians always ask for – our prayers. Pray also for those who persecute Christians, that God will change their hearts and draw them to him.
- SUPPORT MINISTRIES THAT champion the cause of the persecuted church.
- PARTICIPATE IN ADVOCACY campaigns.
- STAY INFORMED.
- WHERE APPROPRIATE (AND following clear direction) write to encourage those who are suffering.

Irina Ratushinskaya, raised in cold war atheistic Russia, was converted to Christ through her experience of the beauty of snow and reading Russian classics. Through the writings of Dostoevsky, Pushkin, Turgenev and Tolstoy she found a real sense of a loving God. She did not see a Bible until she was 23 years old. As a Christian poet, she was marked out as an enemy of the state, and sentenced to seven years hard labour and seven years in internal exile and sent to Barashevo camp in Mordavia, in the Soviet Union's notorious Gulag. After her release, she found that thousands of Christians worldwide had been praying for her, and related the effects of those prayers in her book, *Pencil Letter*.

> Believe me, it was often thus
> In solitary cells, on winter nights
> A sudden sense of joy and warmth
> And a resounding note of love.
> And then, unsleeping, I would know
> A-huddle by an icy wall:
> Someone is thinking of me now,
> Petitioning the Lord for me.
> My dear ones, thank you all
> Who did not falter, who believed in us!
> In the most fearful prison hour
> We probably would not have passed
> Through everything – from end to end,
> Our heads held high, unbowed –
> Without your valiant hearts to light our path.[193]

## Pause for Prayer

We give thanks to you, Father of
the One Family of God.

Once, we were dead, but now have been made
alive with Christ, your new creation people.

Once we were outcasts, but now we
sit the top table of your grace.

Once we were alone, but we have come in
from the cold, to sit at the fireside of your
love; joined with you, and joined together.

Through us, may love's call reach those
still frozen in fear, and draw them in.

Through us, may unity and mercy be
modelled, a winsome demonstration of
how life was always meant to be.

Help us to truly honour each other.

Help us celebrate our differences, and not
fear them or be threatened by them.

Help us gather around what we truly share.

Strengthen those who suffer simply because they love
your Name; bring comfort, hope, justice, and freedom.

In the Name of Christ we pray.

Amen.

## Suggested reading

**The Challenge of Jesus – NT Wright, SPCK**

How DID JESUS understand his own identity and
mission?

**The Provocative Church – Graham Tomlin, SPCK**

TOMLIN SHOWS HOW God's purposes are fulfilled
through the creation of a prophetic community, and
how the implications of that call for mission.

# 5 ONE PEOPLE: IN THE NEW TESTAMENT

APOSTOLIC

One Holy, Catholic, Apostolic People

Then the eleven disciples went to Galilee, to the mountain where Jesus had told them to go. When they saw him, they worshipped him; **but some doubted**. Then Jesus came to them and said, 'All **authority in heaven and on earth has been given to me. Therefore go** and **make disciples** of all nations, **baptising** them in the name of the Father and of the Son and of the Holy Spirit, and **teaching** them to obey everything I have commanded you. And surely I am with you always, to the very end of the age.' – *Matthew 28:16–20*

# 5 ONE PEOPLE: IN THE NEW TESTAMENT

## 1

### Teaching Block 1:

### Travelling Light

Teaching Block 1: Our aim is to uncover the sense that the People of God are a travelling, flawed global community moving to a glorious destination and look into how this will affect how we can often see ourselves and how others see us.

We shall read and discuss the Great Commission with a deeper understanding of what was being asked of the People of God and how we can respond.
We shall explore the need and meaning in the rituals that mark our identity rather than halt our progress in the journey.

## 2

### Teaching Block 2:

### The Mission of God

Teaching Block 2: Our aim is to understand the breadth of our mission by dispelling wrong assumptions that have grown up around mission and evangelism (please note the defining comments at the end of each 'myth').

We shall develop and challenge our ideas of how conversion takes place and the implications for the church and its mission.

## 3

### Teaching Block 3:

### Sent to make Disciples

Teaching Block 3: Our aim is to understand the early theological development of the process of 'catechesis' that relied on quality teaching from acclaimed teachers.
We shall investigate the implications of this for the leadership of the local, national and international church.

We shall look at the difference between a convert and a disciple and how the current dominating practices and learning processes of your church and the UK church shape the People of God for good and ill.

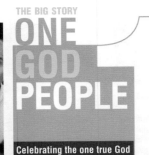

# One Holy, Catholic, Apostolic People – the People of God in Paul and other New Testament writers

# Introduction

## Prelude: Summit meeting

Perhaps Peter and John thought they'd seen it all. Peter knew what it was to look at water that would, for a few seconds at least, support his weight. They'd watched blind eyes long clouded and opaque become clear at a word from Jesus. They'd even had a front row view of the nose-wrinkling, jaw-dropping resurrection of stinking Lazarus. And the transfiguration scene, where a literally dazzling Jesus had chatted with none other than Moses and Elijah, had perhaps been the summit of their mountaintop experiences with the Messiah. But now, as the resurrected Jesus stood before them, there were no gabbled words from Peter, no suggestions to build a tent to shelter them all: these apostles all worshipped.

And some doubted. Despite all they'd learned and witnessed, doubt still snapped at their heels. Their brains protested at the message from their eyes, unable to comprehend the image of their dead master now raised – but more that that, the one in charge of everything.

He was announcing that he had all authority, in heaven and earth: everywhere. And he was calling them to go; not to just little Israel, but to the nations; again, everywhere. And then he promised; not just occasional summit meetings like this, but his presence with them *always*: they would never be without him again, not for a second. **He was both sending them and promising to go with them as they went. They were an *apostolic* people.**

So today, we consider:

- **THE DYNAMIC TRUTH that we are a sent people.**
- **OUR MISSION, WHICH is to live authentic lives that are an event that requires an evangelistic explanation. How can we carry the good news?**
- **DISCIPLE MAKING – is it a lost art?**

## Pause for prayer

Mighty God,

You send, and yet come with us

You delegate, and yet are at our side

You reign, and yet we doubt

You call, and still we hesitate.

We would only go, if you will come too

We would only speak, if your power
accompanies our words

We can only be, if you will be with us.

With you, through you, is life.

Without you, there is nothing.

Stay with us, and when all changes, comfort us
with the knowledge of your unchanging love.

We pray in the name of Christ.

Amen.

# Teaching Block 1:

# Travelling Light

## The sent, travelling community

Some are shocked at Matthew – who wrote his gospel for a Jewish audience – so explicitly recording that the good news was to be taken beyond Israel's borders to the entire world. The whole thrust of the episode of 'the great commission' is that the church is always called to be a *sent, travelling people*. The mobile nature of the people of God as portrayed in the New Testament is disclosed by a closer look at the Greek words translated as *apostolic* and *church*.

There are many occurrences of the Greek word *apostolos* in the New Testament, most in the writings of Luke and Paul. It derives from the very common verb *apostellō*, 'to send'. Jesus is an apostle, the Sent One of God (Heb 3:1). Those sent by God to preach to Israel are apostles (Luke 11:49) as are those sent by churches (2 Cor 8:23; Phil 2:25), and of course those sent as 'gifts from God' to lead the church. Ephesians is where most Christians would see a spelling out of apostolic ministry in all of its facets (Eph 4:11–16). Some parts of the church have been preoccupied with defining apostolic succession in relationship to tactile transmission – succession through the laying on of hands. Scripture seems to lead us in the direction of understanding apostolic succession as faithfulness to apostolic teaching and to the core biblical essentials of what makes the church truly the church.

As we saw on Day 2, the word 'church' comes from the word *ekklesia*, a dynamic group on the move with the Lord at their helm. 'The assembly in the desert', as Stephen describes them (Acts 7:38).

Thus apostolic church is a sent, migrating group, travelling together to a glorious destination under God's bidding.

"God's people need only two things: support for the road, and a destination at the end of it." – *John Power*[194]

"God's people are permanently underway, towards the end of the world and the end of time." – *J.C. Hoekendijk*[195]

"Proclaiming its own transience the church pilgrimages towards God's future." – *Werner Kohler*[196]

But this sent people are far from perfect…

## Sent, but flawed…

"When they saw him, they worshipped him; but some doubted." – *Matthew 28:17*

As we look at the writing and practices of the early church, there is a real danger of viewing them through rose-tinted glasses and painting a picture of a nearly-perfect early church that never existed. Just as we are still in process as individuals, so the church is in process as the people of God under construction; it is often more like a building site than a beautiful edifice or 'spiritual house' (1 Peter 2:4,5). The analogy of a house being slowly constructed – hinting of the messiness of such a project – is repeated (Acts 15:14–18, Eph 2:19–22, 2 Cor 6:16, 1 Cor 3:10–17).

# 5 ONE PEOPLE:
# IN THE NEW TESTAMENT

"The face of the church is the face of the sinner." — *Martin Luther*

"The problem of how an unholy concourse of sinful men and women can be in truth the body of Christ is the same as the problem of how a sinful (hu)man can at the same time be accepted as a child of God. … Our present situation arises precisely from the fact that this fundamental insight which the Reformers apply to the position of the Christian individual was not followed through in its application to the nature of the Christian church." — *Lesslie Newbigin*[197]

**The disciple-makers never ceased to be disciples. The word disciple, which carries the idea of an apprentice, speaks of an extended learning experience.** And some lessons took longer to learn than others – the acceptance of Gentile Christians being one.

The apostolic commission given by Jesus was go to *all nations*. But it took time for the disciples to grow into this understanding; so when Gentiles begin to experience the obvious activity of the Spirit and turn to Christ, a crisis broke out in the church. What had clearly been revealed took a considerable time to be worked out in understanding and practice. **The post-Pentecost disciples were not 'turbo-charged' versions of their earlier weak selves, but were still on a journey of growth and understanding.**

We have the letters of Paul and others because of the problems and challenges they faced; corrective teaching was needed to confront real and serious flaws.

- THE CHURCH IN Galatia had a virus of false doctrine, and God's people there were acting like frenzied piranhas, 'biting and devouring each other' (Gal 5:15).
- THE CHRISTIAN COMMUNITIES in Antioch, Jerusalem, Rome, Corinth, Philippi and Thessalonica all experienced tension of one sort or another.
- THE COLOSSIAN CHURCH was under threat from spiritual elitism within the ranks.

- IN CORINTH THERE was chaos from immorality and difficulties around the fundamental issue of the resurrection of the dead.

These were far from perfect churches. But they were apostolic, sent people – people of the Great Commission.

## Health warning

"The narrative [of the Great Commission] is not everybody's favourite Bible passage – over the centuries it has been used and abused for all sorts of disreputable practices." — *John Drane*[198]

When it comes to the words of the Great Commission, theologians agree they are both vitally important and highly dangerous. This is 'the summary of the entire gospel of Matthew' (J. Blank); 'the most important concern of the gospel' (H. Kosmala); 'the 'climax' of the gospel' (U. Luck); and 'a sort of culmination of everything said up until this point' (P. Nepper-Christensen).[199]

"All the threads woven into the fabric of Matthew… draw together here." — *David J. Bosch*[200]

**Misunderstandings of these vital and strategic words have caused terrible pain. Medieval kings used these**

> Tradition is the living faith of the dead – traditionalism is the dead faith of the living.

**words to fuel the Crusades. Conquistadores used them to justify the forced 'conversion' of the native population of South America. They prompted the missionaries of the eighteenth and nineteenth centuries to acts of heroic sacrifice, but also fuelled a nationalist fervour that**

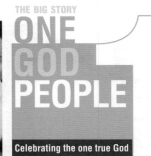
came perilously close to Western imperialism.[201] As we consider the apostolic church and the apostolic commission, we need to tread carefully.

## Diversions, signposts and landmarks: faddism, baptism and eucharist

'Constant change is here to stay,' the saying goes. As we've seen, the church is called to be the people of God on the move. But there are some perils to avoid as we continue on our radical journey. We worship God – not change. We need to steer clear of faddishness, which can so easily divert us from our core mission; and we need to value the signposts and roadmap that God provides for our kingdom trek.

"Then we will no longer be infants, tossed back and forth by the waves, and blown here and there by every wind of teaching."
– *Ephesians 4:14*

"We were therefore buried with him through baptism into death in order that, just as Christ was raised from the dead through the glory of the Father, we too may live a new life."
– *Romans 6:4*

"For I received from the Lord what I also passed on to you: The Lord Jesus, on the night he was betrayed, took bread, and when he had given thanks, he broke it and said, 'This is my body, which is for you; do this in remembrance of me.' In the same way, after supper he took the cup, saying, 'This cup is the new covenant in my blood; do this, whenever you drink it, in remembrance of me.' For whenever you eat this bread and drink this cup, you proclaim the Lord's death until he comes."
– *1 Corinthians 11:23–26*

"The present time is a period in which we may say that the kingdom has come (since it came with the coming of Christ) and yet has still to come because the final consummation is not yet. … In this interim period the church is always looking back and looking forward. That is why the church needs sacraments. And in both baptism and the Lord's supper the church looks back to the death and resurrection of Christ, which have to be reproduced in us, and forward to the full enjoyment of the kingdom."
– *Donald Baillie*[202]

"Tradition is the living faith of the dead as distinct from traditionalism – the dead faith of the living. It is not any old ritual that will do, but respecting the deposit of faith handed on to us by those who have gone before – something much of evangelicalism has lost sight of."
– *Luke Bretherton*[203]

On Day 2 we saw how God reminded his people of 'the big fat story' through various dramatic enactments. It should come as no surprise that Jesus commanded his followers to use the drama of bread and wine shared, an enactment rather than just a verbal rehearsing, and do it 'in remembrance' of him in what Augustine called 'an acted out sermon'.

Eucharist (the act of giving thanks) is also known as the Lord's Supper, Communion and Breaking Bread. All four descriptions find their source in the New Testament. Gathering around the Lord's table is a drama that is unlocked by an understanding of the Passover meal (Exod 12), where a lamb was slaughtered and unleavened bread eaten. Now the Lamb of God would give his body and blood for the sins of the world. As our ancestors savoured the taste of deliverance in the Passover meal, so we are nourished by the feast of freedom that is the Eucharist. **And the burial, resurrection and cleansing that is involved in a person coming to faith in Christ is acted out in the very solid and tangible drama that is the rite of baptism.**

"Baptism and Eucharist are mini-dramas of salvation using material props – water, bread and wine (and in some traditions, juice). By washing a new believer, and by eating and drinking together, Christians use their bodies to re-enact the story of God's gracious salvation in Christ. Through seeing, moving, touching, tasting, and smelling, God speaks again the creative and redeeming Word."
– *Donald McCullough*[204]

# 5 ONE PEOPLE: IN THE NEW TESTAMENT

"The sacraments were intended to establish, strengthen and distinguish the church and to equip her for kingdom life and mission in every age and context."
– T.M. Moore[205]

"Only as the church remembers can it imitate Christ and progress."
– Ian Stackhouse[206]

The mini-dramas of baptism and communion point us back to what *God has done*. Much of our worship centres upon what *God might yet do*, or what we might yet become (or as one writer puts it, 'becoming not what we are'[207]).

This can create a culture of endless angst, especially when it is linked to repeated calls for revival or the next move of the Spirit. God's people totter endlessly (and tiresomely) on the brink of something that might just possibly break out, rather than celebrating the salvation that has already broken out in the finished work of Christ at the Cross. In baptism and communion, we celebrate who we are through what he has done for us. Just as circumcision was a mark of election, not attainment, sacraments point us back to the totality of the work of Christ.

"The weakness of much current work and preaching is that it betrays more of a sense of what has yet to be done than of what has already been done."
– P.T. Forsyth[208]

In baptism and communion, we are not just being faithful to ceremony or delighting that another person has been added to the church; we are actively participating in the power of the story aided by the Holy Spirit, which the catechism calls 'the church's living memory'. This is dynamic remembering, not nostalgia.

"In the light of the resurrection, it is the recalling into the present the very real and substantial events of death and resurrection, in order that they might be celebrated, enjoyed, even participated in."
– J. Macquarrie[209]

"In remembrance of me, then, is no bare historical reflection of the Cross, but a recalling of the crucified and living Christ in such a way that he is personally present in all the fullness and reality of his saving power, and is appropriated by the believers faith."
– Ralph Martin[210]

"Baptism… gives social embodiment and expression to that different place in which justification sets the sinner, the place where the Word is heard and the Supper celebrated. To live under the discipline of the Word and Table is to be one whose way is being altered."
– C.E. Gunton[211]

> The early church 'broke bread' with great frequency, usually early each morning.

And we look forward.

"The Lord's Supper is at once and the same time a remembrance of the death of Christ, and an expectation of the perfect joy with him in the kingdom, which is already in a measure anticipated at each celebration by the experience of his risen living presence. There is no doubt that the first element, which is absolutely fundamental, has been allowed to exclude the other two, and that the modern church has largely lost that forward-looking expectancy and eschatological joy and hope which were characteristic of the early communities."
– A.J.B. Higgins[212]

An exaggerated obsession to build a church that is relevant to the culture could result in a needs-driven church that has no robust theology or effective ecclesiology. We may be able to gather a big crowd, but to what end? Specifically, the

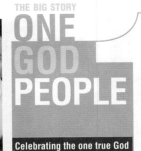

water, bread and wine ensure that we do not forget the bare necessities of the story of the people of God.

- THANKFULNESS IS VITAL; gratitude should be a distinguishing mark of the Christian community.
- THE CHURCH IS a people of repentance and regeneration.
- THE CALL TO follow Christ is a call to participate fully in Christ's community.
- WE ARE A Christocentric (Christ-centred) people – a vital reminder in a day when impersonal metaphors such as wind, river and fire are increasingly used in worship.
- IN CREATION AND incarnation, God was and is vitally interacting with his world and calls us to do the same.
- OUR SALVATION IS rooted in grace, not our accomplishment.
- DISCIPLESHIP IS COSTLY – in baptism, 'we are killed'.[213]
- MISSION IS ROOTED in the actions of the intervening, missionary God, and not in our desperation for the numerical growth of 'our' church.

The early church 'broke bread' with great frequency, usually early each morning. Sunday was not instituted as a public holiday until the fourth century. As we remember, we are refreshed, encouraged and find our imaginations stirred once more.

## Breadsong

It's not in the bread
But in the breaking
That the mystery of God's story is told.
It's not in the seed
But in the dying;
Not in the treasure
But in the digging for it.
It's not in the mountain
But in its moving.

It's not in the wine
But in the pouring out
That a new world is purchased
For the weary.
It's not in the Cross
But in the crucified;
Not in the nails
But the nailing.
It's not in the grave
But in the rising from it.

It's in the giving
That the gift becomes life;
It's in the living
That the word becomes flesh

It's in this taking;
This receiving;
This sharing of a meal,
This pointing to a future
That is promised
And paid for
And pressed into our hands:
It's in this miracle
That the universe is re-born.

*Gerard Kelly*[214]

## So what? Person to Person: For individual reflection

**We've seen that we are sent, but flawed. Sometimes we feel that God is unable to use our lives because of our weakness and brokenness. Reflect on the story of Yitzhak Perlman, arguably the world's greatest violinist.**

Perlman was struck down by polio at the age of twelve; his stumbling walk is aided by crutches and leg braces. At a recent concert at New York's Lincoln Centre, Perlman was set to play an extraordinarily challenging first violin piece that lasted over six minutes. A few seconds into it, the sound of a string breaking on Perlman's violin ricocheted around the hall. The orchestra immediately stopped playing, and the crowd gasped. It would be usual for a musician to go off stage to replace the string – after all, it's quite impossible to play a complicated violin concerto a string short – but because of his disabilities, this changeover would have taken Perlman some time to accomplish. And so he waved the orchestra to continue. Instantly transposing the music for three strings instead of four, Perlman delivered the piece flawlessly, his dancing fingers producing music of unprecedented purity and passion. Six minutes later, soaked in sweat, he lowered his violin.

The crowd sat in stunned silence for eight seconds. And then they rose as one to their feet, a wall of wild cheering and thunderous applause. The orchestra joined in, banging their instruments and shouting themselves hoarse. Perlman called for a microphone, and the man with busted legs and a busted string spoke: 'All my life it has been my mission to make music from that which remains'. He said it twice, and his epic words bear reading again: 'All my life it has been my mission to make music from that which remains.'

And when I heard of his three-stringed virtuosity, I realized that that's what we Christians do best: making music now with what we've got. We hum along with Paul and Silas as they sing their midnight praises in a prison cell; we weep and worship with devastated Jeremiah, we whisper hopeful prayers with barren Hannah, and join in with the magnificent song of the Virgin become Mother who stood shattered on Calvary's hill.

But this is no easy road to walk. Perlman's brilliance is no fluke, but is the fruit of discipline. He practises for nine hours daily. And for forty-five minutes before every concert, Mr. Perlman is found alone in his dressing room. Two security guards stand at the locked door with explicit instructions to let no one in under any circumstances. Mr. Perlman is praying.

Perlman plays hard, and prays harder. We can join him. Let's use what we've got, play the hand we've been dealt and follow the Jesus who stands astride eternity but who seems most interested in today. And as you and I make music with what we have, may we know that even though our ears are mostly deaf to their partying, there are angels cheering us on.[215]

**What music is God calling you to make?**

## So what? People to People: For group discussion together

How can we avoid faddism, and yet embrace innovation, change and risk?

We know that the church is sent, yet flawed. Why do we remain surprised and disappointed at the flaws and weaknesses of the church? How can we remain hopeful and yet realistic?

## Teaching Block 2:

# The Mission of God

### The street preacher

The very word 'evangelism' gives many Christians a shiver, and usually makes most of us feel guilty. The screaming street preacher harassing passers-by with a message that doesn't sound much like good news invokes in us a mixture of emotions.

- WE SENSE THAT the approach is not helpful, and yet perhaps we admire the commitment and dedication.

- WE WORRY BECAUSE we know the gospel is urgently and desperately needed – and so wonder, Should we be out on the streets too?

- WE SENSE THAT we'd like to share our faith with others more, but are not sure how to do it. Some evangelistic training courses make us feel that we're being trained to read a script or push a product, and we're nervous about the 'scalp hunting' feel that some evangelistic initiatives have.

**Evangelism is not a sales programme, with salvation as the marketable product. Vinay Samuel says that evangelism is a commitment to sharing, not an announcement of expected outcomes. And it is not about us 'playing God'.**

❝The greatest danger to wrong headed thinking about evangelism is that we will use evangelism as a way to play God in the lives of other people, believing we know the state of their soul, when they need to say 'yes' to God, or that we know something about their future that they do not."
*– Bryant L. Myers*[216]

### Myths and mission: ten really bad commandments

The subject of mission and evangelism is huge, and could warrant our attention for the entire Spring Harvest week. However, here are ten myths about this subject that we need to expose.

### Myth 1: Mission and evangelism have no place in a postmodern world

We've seen from the beginning of our journey together this week that we are the people of the Big Story; and that the story must be told to the world, which is suffering from a story famine. When we lose our sense of mission, not only does the world lose but the church suffers too. Just as Israel lost her way when she failed to realise her calling to be a lighthouse people, so the church becomes dysfunctional when she loses her mission focus.

❝The [Enlightenment] experiment has failed. It is after the fact obvious that it had to. If there is no universal storyteller, then the universe can have no storyline. Neither you nor I, not all of us together, can so shape this world that it can make narrative sense. If God does not invent the world's story, then it has none. Then the world has no narrative that is its own. If there is no God, or if indeed there is some other God than the God of the Bible, then there is no narratable world."
*– Robert Jenson*[217]

❝The minute the church becomes a club for like-minded people, enjoying vertical privileges and failing to hold out the horizontal invitation to become a disciple of

the King, a member of the kingdom, then it too will lose its identity and direction." – *Graham Tomlin*[218]

**In appraising mission, we must not lose mission.**

## Myth 2: Everything we do is mission anyway

Mission is broad and must not be too tightly confined. Evangelism has unfortunately been differentiated from worship and pastoral care, even though all of them have a clear mission element. In 1965 Donald McGavran, the so-called 'father' of the church growth movement, drew an unhelpful distinction between worship and evangelism: 'Worship is good, but worship is worship. It is not evangelism.'[219]

Surely worship does have a clear mission element to it. As God's people declare his worth and wonder in creed and song, there will be those who are drawn by that charming sound. **But we should also heed the caution that when everything is mission, then nothing is mission.**

A story is told of a bishop in the Church of England who defined evangelism as being whatever we do for church, including mowing the church lawn. While an attractive lawn and a legible notice board might serve the cause of evangelism, because the building looks more attractive to enquirers, nonetheless this should not be confused with evangelism. Graham Tomlin offers a distinction between the words 'mission' and 'evangelism'.

**Mission** = All actions that demonstrate or recall God's rule over the world.

**Evangelism** = Words that explain these actions.[220]

**Mission implies a sense of clear strategy – doing, as well as being.**

## Myth 3: It's up to us to change the world

**Mission is actually not something that we initiate at all – we participate in the *Missio Dei*, the mission of God.** Whenever the church takes an unhealthy responsibility for mission, then things go badly wrong. Mission is God's project, orchestrated and directed by God's spirit: the invitation to us is to be junior partners, not clever initiators.

“The priority for the church is neither evangelism nor social action; it is to live under the lordship of Christ. In other words, the central thing is not a human task, but a divine action. It is not our work of spreading the gospel or changing society, but it is the new reality brought into being by the coming of Christ." – *Graham Tomlin*[221]

“The chief actor in the historic mission of the Christian church is the Holy Spirit. He is the director of the whole enterprise. The mission consists of the things that he is doing in the world." – *John Taylor*[222]

**Above all, we are called into the friendship and love of God.** This is also the priority of the calling of the first apostles; the twelve are called to 'be with him' (Mark 3:14). The pivotal moment of Mark's Gospel is the apostolic confession that Jesus is the Christ (Mark 8:29); knowing Christ is the apostolic priority, as Paul insists.

“I want to know Christ and the power of his resurrection and the fellowship of sharing in his sufferings, becoming like him in his death, and so, somehow, to attain to the resurrection from the dead." – *Philippians 3:10–11*

The promise of Jesus that he would 'be with' the sent people of God is of course fulfilled through the ministry of the Holy Spirit. John 14–17 unpacks the great commissioning discourse of the Twelve. Their commission from Jesus is as real as his from God (cf. John 20:21); they are to bear witness from their long acquaintance with Jesus, yet the Spirit bears witness of him (John 15:26–27). He will remind them of the words of Jesus (John 14:26), and guide them into all the truth and show them the age to come (of the church)

# 5 ONE PEOPLE: IN THE NEW TESTAMENT

and Christ's glory (John 16:13–15). The apostolic commission and empowering of the Spirit to fulfil that commission are completely entwined.

Emphasis in recent years on experiencing the power of the Holy Spirit means we should once again remember that the Spirit is a divine *person*, not an impersonal force; the pronouns of the Spirit in the New Testament are interpreted as personal pronouns. Without the activity of the Holy Spirit, there is no true mission, because the mission of God must be initiated and choreographed by the life-giving one who is the Holy Spirit.

**The people of God are sent by God on God's mission, sent with God, and filled with God's spirit.**

## Myth 4: Everyone must tell their friends (and passing strangers) about Jesus

Christian leaders often exhort everyone in their congregation to get out and tell their friends the gospel – but the New Testament contains few appeals that we should actually do this. That isn't to suggest that the vital mission imperative doesn't sit at the heart of the New Testament – it is rather that **the focus of Paul and other New Testament writers is to get the mission *community* functioning effectively as those who live provocatively, rather than mobilizing individual spokespersons to announce the gospel**. The letters to Ephesians is one example: here is the purpose of God for his people from creation to end times – and yet evangelism is not mentioned, except in Paul's appeal for prayer that he might make a bold proclamation of the message in his own ministry and calling.

So why is it that 'personal' evangelism is not mentioned more? The answer often given is that there was a basic assumption that every Christian would function in this way – but at best, this is an argument from silence. Of course all believers are called to be witnesses for Christ – but that does not necessarily imply that all will be functioning as *evangelists*, with a specific gift of sharing the gospel and helping others to do so.

"Why doesn't… the New Testament mention evangelism more often? The answer is surely that the church's first task is to be what it is meant to be, to display the wisdom of God to whoever looks in from the outside. This new community is called to demonstrate, by the distinctiveness of its life and the harmony created among very different people, God's variegated wisdom. The task is to learn to live the Christian life

**Without actions, no one listens. Without words, no one understands.**

before we talk about it; to walk the walk, before we talk the talk. God has chosen to work out his will for the world not through a bunch of individuals being sent out to persuade others to believe in him, but by creating a new community made up of very different people, giving them his Spirit who enables them to live together in unity, to develop a new way of life and to live this way of life publicly. Evangelism then finds its place within this context. Even though it isn't highlighted as the highest priority of every Christian, evangelists are still key figures within the local church. The role of the evangelist (Paul himself is a prime example) is to articulate on behalf of the rest of the community the invitation to come under God's rule."
– *Graham Tomlin*[223]

**Mission is often best expressed by the community of God doing what it does best – being a community of Christ; a mission responsibility shared together.**

## Myth 5: We must initiate every conversation about God

> "But in your hearts set apart Christ as Lord. Always be prepared to give an answer to everyone who asks you to give the reason for the hope that you have."
> — *1 Peter 3:15*

> "What does this mean?"
> — *Acts 2:12*

**Evangelism is often the second act of the story. If we live provocatively and dynamically as Christians, our lifestyles will provoke those around to ask why it is that we live as we do. Thus we see a process of event-question-answer.**

Peter picks up this idea as he encourages us to always be ready to give a reason for the hope that we have – and the giving of a *reason* implies that someone has asked a *question*. We see this pattern on the Day of Pentecost: Peter is giving an explanation that is in response to the crowd's question, 'What does this mean?' The same pattern is shown when the man is healed at Solomon's Colonnade (Acts 3:11). Also, Stephen does miracles and then 'preaches' in response to the enquiry made, or in his case, the interrogatory question (Acts 7:1). In each case, there was an event that required an explanation, and the gospel was the explanation. Paul Tillich complains that so much evangelism is about 'throwing answers, like stones, at the heads of those who haven't even asked a question.'[224]

> "Something has happened which makes people aware of a new reality, and therefore the question arises: What is this reality? The communication of the gospel is the answering of that question."
> — *Lesslie Newbigin*[225]

Pachomius was an Egyptian who in the early years of the fourth century AD was conscripted into the Roman army. He was taken down the Nile to a place near Luxor that was a kind of cross between a prison and an army barracks, where he was visited by a strange group of local people with gifts of food and drink. Intrigued, he asked why they would come to visit someone they didn't know and had no

obligation to. The answer was that it was because they were followers of Jesus and had a custom of visiting those in prison as they would visit Jesus himself, just as their Lord had taught them. Pachomius was so impressed by these 'Christians' he decided to become one of them. In time, he became one of the most important founders of communal Christian monasticism, the movement that served to keep Christianity alive during many of the dark days to come after the fall of the Roman Empire.
— Graham Tomlin[226]

**Sometimes we rush to give answers before a question has been asked.**

## Myth 6: Just live the life, and never open your mouth

This is the opposite of Myth 5. In recent years preachers have made use of a popular phrase, usually attributed to St. Francis of Assisi – 'Travel everywhere, preach the gospel, and use words if you have to.' This can lead us to an unbalanced view of what evangelism is, as if we should never open our mouth. Francis sold everything and gave all he had to the poor – a somewhat extreme and wonderfully radical lifestyle that was rather arresting. And of course Jesus *did* more than he *said*, often activating a search in those who witnessed his actions rather than simply just explaining them immediately. **But evangelism will usually involve verbal explanation; this seems consistent with the Greek word *euangelizomai*, which always seems to bear a verbal content.**

> "Without actions, no one listens. Without words, no one understands."
> — *Graham Tomlin*[227]

Healings, as marvellous as they are, require an explanation. They startle, but do not necessarily inform, and can be wrongly interpreted. Just as some in Jesus day assigned his power to a satanic source.

> "Healings, even the most wonderful, do not call this present world radically into question; the gospel does and this has to be made explicit."
> — *Lesslie Newbigin*[228]

# 5 ONE PEOPLE: IN THE NEW TESTAMENT

Vincent Donovan describes the strategy of the Catholic mission among the Masai in Tanzania. Sensing that the Masai were not ready to hear a clear verbal presentation of the gospel message, the decision was made to serve the people in concrete terms, mission through service, and they would eventually come to faith as a result. This failed, and the decision was made to go to the village elders and talk about faith. The response from the elders was immediate: 'If this is why you came here, why did you wait so long to tell us about this?'[229]

Muslims in West Africa criticized Christian development workers because they were so reluctant to speak about their faith. One of them laid out the challenge: 'Don't put up your own ghosts. Speak what you believe!'

**Let's not replace evangelistic verbosity with silence. Evangelism demands that we sensitively verbalise the message as is appropriate.**

## Myth 7: We just need more seeker-sensitive events

The idea of a seeker-sensitive church has caused many of us to ask helpful questions about how visitors perceive us, questions that address a biblical concern (1 Cor 14: 23–25). **But mission is surely about the church being herself. Sometimes the church excessively 'targets' newcomers in special services, making them feel more like potential scalps.** A member of a small group advised fellow members that a Buddhist friend would be attending. The group turned its guns on the hapless visitor and 'the conversion of this one man became the focus of the meeting, not Christ.'[230] Not surprisingly, the Buddhist went away bruised and damaged – and never returned. William Beckham suggests a better way for small groups.

"The meeting format should not be changed to convert them or focus on them. They should be allowed to sit and watch God at work in his people. … The New Testament church knew the most powerful witness was the community of believers living in the presence, power and purpose of Christ. … Through the imper-

fection of Christians, God reveals his power to those who observe."
– *William Beckham*[231]

The story of Derek Draper,[232] a successful political lobbyist who was forced to resign from government work following a public scandal, demonstrates how 'the church being about her business' can be winsome and attractive.

"That Sunday, I walked into a church service for the first time since I was thirteen. I had stumbled upon the perfect church for me. … The splendour of the robes, the incense and the beautiful choir mix with an informality that was summed up on All Saints Day, when two altar boys mounted the steps with day-glo trainers showing under their vestments. That first Sunday, the vicar managed to combine a sermon addressing fear with a genuinely funny joke… I was hooked."[233]

"When the church begins to be truly itself, it will not be able to stop itself being evangelistic."
– *Graham Tomlin*[234]

"Training in evangelism should mention that one of the simplest and most effective forms of evangelism is, 'Would you like to come to church with me next Sunday?'"
– *John Finney*

"The spiritual journey – conversion – is about people being caught up into the presence of God, and responding in ways that will move them on towards that total commitment to Christ which, according to the New Testament, is at the heart of discipleship. Worship plays a key role in that kind of faith journey… effective evangelism and renewed worship are inextricably linked."
– *John Drane*[235]

**That is not to say that 'seeker sensitive' events shouldn't be used. But if we run them, let them be filled with content that is sensitive and winsome.**

## Myth 8: Everyone needs to be dynamically converted

With the emergence of *Alpha*, there has been an increasing awareness that conversion is more usually a process rather than a crisis. Does this conflict with traditional understandings of a sudden 'Damascus Road' conversion like that of Saul of Tarsus or St Augustine, who, having heard a voice in a Milan garden, read Paul's letters and was converted there and then? New Testament imagery also speaks of dramatic change – moving from death to life, being born again, and stepping from darkness in light.

**Most people report that their conversion was a process rather than a crisis** – 69 per cent, according to John Finney's now famous 1992 survey.

**"**While [conversion] can be triggered by particular events, and, in some cases result in very sudden experiences of change, for the most part [conversion] takes place over a period of time." – *Lewis Rambo*[236]

Saul, the classic model of sudden conversion, already had a considerable knowledge of biblical revelation because of his training as a Pharisee, and also had witnessed the stoning of Stephen.

**Surely we can hold to the biblical imagery of conversion without insisting that this necessarily takes place at a recorded moment. We acknowledge that even in the crisis imagery of 'new birth' that the process of bringing forth new life happened long before anyone stepped into the labour ward.**

**"**Too much 'process' and the distinctiveness and assurance of being a Christian may be lost. Too much 'crisis' and we may end up forcing people into a mould that they don't fit. 'Process' courses in evangelism also need to make space for 'crisis' moments. Transformation needs to make space for regeneration in the course of conversion." – *Graham Tomlin*[237]

**"**The gradual process is the way in which the majority of people discover God, and the average time taken is about four years: models of evangelism which can help people along the pathway are needed." – *John Finney*[238]

**Let's acknowledge and celebrate the truth that conversion is about *process and crisis*.**

> **Mission is therefore not something that we do, but is the heartbeat of our life together.**

## Myth 9: The goal of evangelism is to get everyone to 'invite Jesus into their hearts'

Although it's increasingly rare these days, some people still seem to think that evangelism is about getting as many people as possible to pray 'a sinner's prayer'. **The Christian message is a call to invite people to come under the kingdom reign and rule of Christ and become his followers. Jesus' evangelism was kingdom evangelisation.**[239]

**"**Evangelism announces the liberating work of God as in Christ he fashions a new humanity." – *Harvie Conn*[240]

**The invitation of true mission is not just to sign on the dotted line for salvation insurance; mission is the invitation to all to come and be a part of the kingdom community.**

## Myth 10: We the church don't have to change to be effective in mission

As we have considered today that we are a travelling people, following Christ into change, rather than worshipping or revering change itself, we must also reflect soberly lest we become a church that refuses to change.

One church in the UK holds an annual meeting called 'The Ichabod Meeting'. The word 'ichabod' means 'the glory has departed' (1 Sam 4:21). The church asks the hard question, Which of our activities are showing no evidence of blessing and usefulness? Instead of perpetuating time- and money-consuming activities that produce little, that church has been willing to ask the difficult questions in order to become more effective.[241]

**Our mission must create our shape, rather than trying to fit mission into our current shape.**

**Mission is therefore not something that we do, but is the heartbeat of our life together. As we make ourselves available to God the missionary, and with his help live in a way that will require explanation, and as we make the changes that mission will demand, so then we will truly be a lighthouse people.**

## Mission and the Hope Project

The churches of the United Kingdom and Northern Ireland are on a constant mission to serve and witness to the 56 million people who inhabit the complex and multi-layered communities that lie within these isles. A new initiative called Hope (www.hope08.com) is seeking to support this on-going work by facilitating a year of intensified, united, focused prayer and activities, communicating the gospel through words and actions, and creating a lasting legacy of both physical and spiritual change in the lives of communities and individuals. Hope's vision is to act as a catalyst to encourage, support and resource churches in 'raising their game' to better serve the communities they are called to reach.

Hope is a grassroots initiative, supporting local churches to engage with their communities through words and actions, with prayer having a central place. It wants to encourage collaborative activities between churches of all traditions and backgrounds, and also wants to encourage collaboration between churches and agencies in reaching out to their communities.

Through resourcing and training and the encouragement of good practice, to develop the ability of churches to engage with their communities in the long term, Hope is looking to help the church realise a dream: thousands of individuals and communities being impacted by the gospel through words and actions.

There will be:

- MAJOR CITY-WIDE MISSIONS over the summer of 2008 in Glasgow, London, Birmingham, Manchester, Merseyside, Cardiff and Belfast. These will develop as flagship events, carrying their own identity but linked with the Hope vision and brand.

- SUPPORT FOR CHURCHES to use either a weekend or a week during the summer for focused missional activities into their communities. Hope will look to provide resources to support and cohesion through identification with a national initiative.

- ENCOURAGEMENT TOWARDS GOOD news through action, which might include rubbish clearance, graffiti cleaning, parkland reclamation, football tournaments, and sports and arts academies.

- ENCOURAGEMENT TOWARDS SHARING good news through words, including concerts, community barbecues, children's clubs, celebrations, street teams, workplace initiatives, visits to retirement homes, and Alpha Suppers.

## So what? Person to Person: For individual reflection

Welsh poet R.S. Thomas paints a haunting portrait in 'The Chapel' of a Christian group that once was dynamic and effective, but now has settled into benign ineffectiveness.

A little aside from the main road
becalmed in a last century greyness
there is the chapel, ugly, without the appeal
to the tourist to stop his car
and visit it. The traffic goes by,
and the river goes by, and quick shadows
of clouds too, and the chapel settles
a little deeper into the grass.

But here once on an evening like this
in the darkness that was about
his hearers, a preacher caught fire
and burned steadily before them
with a strange light, so that they saw
the splendour of the barren mountains
about them and sang their amens
fiercely, narrow but saved
in a way that men are not now.[242]

How do dynamic churches end up settling a little deeper in the grass? Have you and I at times championed things staying the same, and therefore contributed to that settling? Are we fighting change that we should be supporting?

## So what? People to People: For group discussion together

Graham Tomlin calls us to be a 'provocative' church. What are some of the characteristics of being a provocative people that might create a reaction of interest in your community?

Mission demands change, and the very essence of being sent people means that we will have to navigate through changing scenery and seasons. Why do Christians find change such a challenge? What has been one area of change that has created conflict in your church? How was the conflict resolved?

3 Teaching Block 3:

# Sent to make disciples

## The Travellers: All Apprentices

"I press on toward the goal to win the prize for which God has called me heavenward in Christ Jesus."
— *Philippians 3:14*

"My dear children, for whom I am again in the pains of childbirth until Christ is formed in you."
— *Galatians 4:19*

"But grow in the grace and knowledge of our Lord and Saviour Jesus Christ."
— *2 Peter 3:18*

"We need to create church communities that make disciples, equipped both to live the message as well as share it. This after all was Jesus' method. He did not say, 'Go and make converts.' He said: 'Go and make disciples of all nations' (Matt 28:19). So, if we want to change our communities, we have to change our values and ask ourselves two vital questions. Are we a *whole-life* community – committed to addressing all of life? A community for whom there is no sacred-secular divide. One people whose understanding of God's comprehensive interest in all of life is helping them make a difference wherever they are and whatever they do. And are we a *disciple-making* community: an apprentice community committed to developing the kinds of relationships and skills to genuinely help one another live, grow and flourish in Christ – through all the seasons of life?"
— *Mark Greene*

"The early church sets for us a challenging example on how to train new believers and help them grow in Christ during the first three years of their walk with the Lord. It is my hope that evangelical churches would invest more time, thought, prayer, planning, and resources into a healthy assimilation of new believers."
— *Clinton E. Arnold*[243]

Visit www.licc.org.uk/imagine

When we consider how the Christian church in the first four centuries developed a process for 'sound conversion', we must be challenged by their rigorous plan and commitment to ground new believers in their Christian lives. The early church gave themselves to the training of new believers – a practice they called *catechumenate*, from the Greek word *katechein* (meaning 'to teach' or 'instruct'). Becoming fully integrated into the life of the church community was a lengthy process. As the early church developed and matured there is evidence of a focused and coherent plan to instruct new believers. Some of the structure and content of the catechumenate may have been influenced by the Jewish procedure for training proselytes.

"When the heathen desire and promise to repent, saying 'We believe,' we receive them into the congregation so that they may hear the word, but do not receive them into communion until they receive the seal and are fully initiated."
— *Didascalia Apostolorum*[244]

Some elements of the process were as follows:

- **THOSE WHO LED catechumenate groups had a deep love for the people in their care.** St. Augustine advised his friend Deogratias about how to carry out his teaching responsibilities with the catechumens. 'We should endeavour to meet them with a brother's, a father's, and a mother's love' and seek to be 'united with them thus in heart'.[245]

New Christians are not prospects or projects but real people with stories. They are not to be processed but cared for.

- **THE CATECHUMENS WERE able to count the cost of faith, and make a clear, thoughtful and considered commitment to follow Christ.** It is often taught that the early church immediately baptised their converts, and so we should do likewise, but in fact this practice ceased fairly quickly. Perhaps the most significant motive for the shift away from the early apostolic practice of baptising immediately after profession of faith to delaying baptism until after substantive training, mentoring and preparation had to do with 'the concern the ministers of baptism had from the very beginning for the sincerity of the conversion of the candidates.'[246] By the second century the church had developed a lengthy catechumenate that it required candidates to complete prior to baptism: this was perhaps because most first-century converts were Jews or god-fearers, but second-century converts were pagans who needed extensive instruction and resocialisation. The longer catechetical process was also a result of the theological disputes present in the second century. In an age of persecution, there was a need to 'screen out' possible spies and informers, and the teachings of Jesus required significant time to imbibe and practise.

Are we guilty of rushing people into public confessions of faith before they are ready to make that commitment?

- **THEY TOOK THEIR time.** We discover that the training often took place over a three-year span.[247] The Apostolic

Tradition:[248] 'Let the catechumens hear the Word for three years.' Part of the motivation for a lengthy process was a desire to foster solid spiritual formation and to protect these new believers against major sin, heresy, and apostasy.

"The key was conversion, itself a journey, or as the ancients put it, a change ('turning from one "way of walking" to another')." – *Thomas Finn*[249]

Are we willing to take the time and make the effort to create a 'nursery' environment for new Christians?

- **THEY INVESTED THEIR best teachers.** As we consider the lives and writings of the most well-known church leaders in the first four centuries, it is amazing how many of them were devoted to teaching new believers. Origen (185–254), a great scholar, had a passionate concern for training new believers in the Scriptures and grounding in the faith – and he was a very popular teacher.

"This astonishingly dynamic man [Origen] never ceased to concern himself with the seriousness of baptismal formation. In the expanding church of his time, it hurt him to see numbers threatening to submerge quality, and he struggled for the purity of the Christian life as it was during the second century." – *Michel Dujarer*[250]

Other heavyweights of church history who were heavily involved in the catechumenate include Tertullian, who had an 'abiding and passionate concern for the formation of catechumens',[251] Hippolytus (Rome; 170–236), Ambrose (Italy; 339–97), Cyprian (North Africa; d. 258), Gregory of Nyssa (Asia Minor; 330–395), John Chrysostom (Byzantium; 347–407), and many others. One other important figure is Augustine. In Hippo, North Africa, one of his responsibilities was director of a catechumenate. One of Augustine's most important works, providing insight into the fourth-century catechumenate, is a document called *De Catechizandis Rudibus*, 'On the Catechizing of the Uninstructed.'

**If the training of new believers was such an important ministry in the estimation of the well-known leaders and teachers of the ancient church, it is natural to ask whether it is equally a priority among the scholars and Bible teachers of our time.**

"Let me compare the catechizing to a building. Unless we methodically bind and joint the whole structure together, we shall have leaks and dry rot, and all our previous exertions will be wasted." – *Cyril of Jerusalem*[252]

- **THE CATECHUMENS WERE immersed in the Scriptures.** At the heart of the early church catechumenate was reading and instructing newcomers in Scripture. The first line of *The Apostolic Tradition* that describes the catechumenate characterises the catechumens as those who are brought 'to hear the Word'. We assume that vast portions of Scripture were read to the new believers. But it was also a time where teachers would provide explanations of Scripture. This procedure is certainly modeled by Origen in his ministry at Caesarea. The church there held a daily service of the Word in which a large passage of Scripture would be read aloud followed by a sermon delivered by Origen. In some places, the catechumens gathered together early in the morning before going to work for Scripture reading, teaching, and prayer. This practice is described in *The Apostolic Tradition*.[253]

**Are we genuinely a biblically literate people and do we resource new Christians to know the full revelation of Scripture?**

- **BIG STORY teaching.** In his work on the catechizing of the uninstructed, Augustine strongly emphasizes how important it is for the teacher to lay out the broad sweep of salvation history.

"The narration is full when each person is catechised in the first instance from what is written in the text, 'In the beginning God created the heaven and the earth,' on to the present times of the church…. What we ought to do is, to give a comprehensive statement of all things, summarily and generally, so that certain of the more wonderful facts may be selected which are listened to with superior gratification, and which have been ranked so remarkably among the exact turning-points (of the history)."
– *Augustine (De Catechizandis Rudibus 3.6)*

Augustine here advocates something similar to what we might call a Bible survey class in a modern curriculum. He is advocating this instruction for every new Christian.

**Do we give new Christians the headlines of the faith or the big picture? At the beginning of our journey we considered that we often forget the 'Big Fat Story of God'. Is it possible that we ourselves have never learned it in the first place?**

- **CREED AND SCRIPTURE were both prioritised.** In addition to teaching scripture, the teachers of the catechumenate bore the responsibility for passing on and explaining the central doctrines of the faith. In Jerusalem catechumens formally received the creed after weeks of hearing the Scriptures.[254]

"While creedal phrases charted the main lines of this catechetical edifice, biblical stories shaped its interior … Cyril linked creed and Scriptures in a complex fashion." – *William Harmless*[255]

In reflecting on the catechetical instruction that he received at the beginning of his Christian life, Theodoret (393–460) describes how he learned the Holy Scriptures and received what he now believes, declares, and teaches. He then recites the Nicene Creed and other creedal statements.

Catechetical instruction not only involved hearing scripture, but also learning the common confession of the church as summarised in the creed. The tendency for the church to begin summarising the heart of the faith in propositional statements began at the earliest stages as seen, for instance, in Paul's appeal to common creedal confession in 1 Corinthians 15:3–4. The focus on learning doctrine has

long been a part of a common understanding of catechism in Catholic and Protestant circles. Memorisation of the creed was probably the main form of catechesis in the middle ages.[256]

**Do churches that do not use liturgy need to find ways to become confessing churches that consistently and corporately declare their faith?**

- SPIRITUAL AND MORAL **formation.** Another common theme that emerges in descriptions of the ancient church catechumenate is the renunciation of sinful life-styles and the cultivation of Christian character. The early church leaders were quite admonitory, direct and uncompromising with the catechumens with regard to their lifestyles.

**Are we ready for preaching that will address the difficult and sometimes intimate issues of everyday life?**

- DELIVERANCE MINISTRY. ONE of the common and widespread characteristics of the ancient church catechumenate was what we might call 'deliverance ministry'. New believers were expected to clearly renounce Satan and received prayer for freedom from dark influences, especially around the time of baptism.

"And when the days approach [for the occasion of baptism], let the bishop exorcise each one of them separately by himself, so that he may be persuaded that he is pure. For if there be one that is not pure, or in whom is an unclean spirit, let him be reproved by that unclean spirit. If then anyone is found under any such suspicion, let him be removed from

the midst [of them], and let him be reproved and reproached because he has not heard the word of the commandments and of instruction faithfully, because the evil and strange spirit remained in him."
*– Testamentum Domini (2.6)*

"And a deacon shall take the oil of exorcism and stand at the left hand of the presbyter…. And when the presbyter grasps each one of those who will receive baptism, let him command him to renounce, saying, 'I renounce you, Satan, with all your service and all your works.' And when he has renounced all these, let him anoint him with the oil of exorcism, saying, 'Let every spirit be cast far from you.'"
*– The Apostolic Tradition (21.8–10)*

Immediately following this exorcism and renunciation of Satan, the person being baptised would confess their allegiance to Christ in a creedal form.

"I believe in the only true God, the Father, the Almighty, and his only begotten Son, Jesus Christ our Lord and Saviour with his Holy Spirit, the giver of life to everything, three in one substance (*homoousios*), one divinity, one lordship, one kingdom, one faith, one baptism, in the holy catholic apostolic church, which lives forever. Amen."
*– The Apostolic Tradition (21.12)*

Anglicans will be familiar with the practice of 'renouncing Satan' in the liturgy surrounding baptism.

**Will we live as the people of God, rather than people of darkness, and call others to clearly live as people of the light?**

## A last word: people of God, people of hope

We began our journey by reminding ourselves that we are the people of the 'Big Fat Story of God'. Will we live by that story, or succumb to mere survival? Phillip Greenslade writes (over) specifically about the power of preaching, but his words challenge us more broadly to 'reject the unreal drama'.

"The day is 22nd November 1963. David Lodge, a playwright, is in a playhouse watching one of his creations being performed on stage. There is a scene in the middle of the play where a character, according to the script and demands of the plot, turns on a transistor radio and tunes in to a local station. On this day the theatre is full. The actors are caught up in the drama of their performance – the scripted lines, the choreographed movements, the contrived emotions. The audience is spellbound, pulled into the world wonderfully conjured up before them, when along comes this scene. The character takes the radio and flicks it on: there is a crackle and hiss of static. He dials the tuner, a jumble of noise, voices surge and fade, music blares and stutters, and then, stark and urgent, a voice breaks through. 'Today in Dallas, Texas, President John F. Kennedy was shot and killed'. The actor quickly switches off the radio but it is too late. The reality of the real world has with just a few plain words burst in on the closeted self-created world of a play being staged, and the play is over. This is what preaching will do. Preaching the Big Story of God's redemptive plan… will at some point, by the power of the Spirit, break in upon the unreal drama that people are being sold."

– *Phillip Greenslade*[257]

And that redemptive plan continues to roll out into eternity. It's been said that some Christians are 'too heavenly minded to be of any earthly use'. The fact is that there has never yet been a believer who has been too preoccupied with the wonderful news of eternity spent with Christ. As we draw to the end of our look at the people of God, we remind ourselves that the future is wonderfully bright; election shows us that we have a huge responsibility, and eschatology affirms that what we see now is not the end of things – the kingdom will fully and finally come as the new Jerusalem comes down to earth. The people of God are the people of the living hope.

Next year at Spring Harvest we will explore the final element of our three-year theme "The Big Story: One Hope". The people of God are called to be earthly revolutionaries who know that there's more to life than what we see now. The story is big, not just because it spans human history, but because it is the huge drama of eternity. And we are all invited to join in with the next chapter, which starts today.

"The church is the pilgrim people of God. It is on the move – hastening to the ends of the earth to beseech all to be reconciled to God, hastening to the end of time to meet its Lord who will gather all into one."

– *Lesslie Newbigin*[258]

"And I heard a loud voice from the throne saying, 'Now the dwelling of God is with men, and he will live with them. They will be his people, and God himself will be with them and be their God. He will wipe every tear from their eyes. There will be no more death or mourning or crying or pain, for the old order of things has passed away.'"

– *Revelation 21:1–4*

## Suggested reading

**Transforming Mission** – David Bosch, Alban)
THE MOST THOROUGH examination of mission thinking available – a genuine classic.

**Velvet Elvis** – Rob Bell, Zondervan)
ROB BELL REPAINTS the Christian faith in bold and startling strokes of brilliance. He opens new avenues of faith and thought for Christian discipleship.

THE BIG STORY
ONE
GOD
PEOPLE

Celebrating the one true God

# Endnotes

1. *The Upside Down Kingdom*, Donald Kraybill (Herald Press, 1990), 61

2. Martins' *Study of Palestine* (1975), 78

3. Not all loved the Temple, because it had been built by Herod, and some, like the Essenes, saw it as a symbol of national compromise

4. *Jerusalem in the Time of Jesus*, Joachim Jeremias (Fortress, 1975), 83

5. Others contest this, notably Marcus Borg

6. *The Challenge of Jesus*, N.T. Wright (SPCK, 2000), 19,40

7. *The Provocative Church*, Graham Tomlin (SPCK, 2004), 84

8. *Jesus: Conflict, Holiness and Politics*, Marcus Borg (New York, 1984), 175

9. *The Trivialization of God*, Donald McCullough (NavPress, 1995), 74

10. *The Presence of the Kingdom*, Jacques Ellul, Helmers and Howard (1989)

11. *The Provocative Church*, 26

12. *Spoken Worship*, Gerard Kelly (Grand Rapids: Zondervan, 2007)

13. *The Provocative Church*, 43

14. *The Songlines*, Bruce Chatwin (London: Picador, 1987), 72

15. *Threshold of the Future: Reforming the Church in the Post-Christian West*, Michael Riddell (London: SPCK, 1998), 137

16. *The Last Battle*, C.S. Lewis, Book 7 in *The Chronicles of Narnia*, (New York: Macmillan, 1970), 184

17. *Scripture and the Authority of God*, N.T. Wright (SPCK, 2005), 89-93

18. *Walking with the Poor: Principles and Practices of Transformational Development*, Bryant L. Myers (Orbis Books/World Vision, 2002), 23

19. *The Holy Spirit in Today's World*, David Hubbard (Word, 1973), 29

20. *The Dark Interval: Towards a Theology of Story*, John Dominic Crossman (Polebridge Press Westar Institute, US, 1988, 1994)

21. *The Provocative Church*, 9

22. Jean Baudrillard, 'Simulacra and Simulation' in Modernisms/Postmodernisms, Peter Brooker ed. (Longman, 1992), 159

23. *Bridget Jones: The Edge of Reason*, Helen Fielding (Picador, 2000), 142

24. Ted Koppel, quoted in *Harper's Bazaar* (January 1986)

25. *The Meaning of Life*, David Friend (Boston: Little Brown, 1991), 90

26. *God, Creation and Revelation: A Neo-Evangelical Theology*, Paul King Jewett (Eerdmans, 1991), 174

27. Stephen Jay Gould, quoted in *2000 Years of Disbelief: Famous People with the Courage to Doubt*, James A. Haught (Prometheus Books, 1996)

28. *This we Believe*, Ravi Zacharias contrib. (Zondervan, 2000), 29

29. *The Selfish Gene*, Richard Dawkins (St Albans: Granada Publishing, 1978)

30. *The God Delusion*, Richard Dawkins (Bantam Press, Oct 2006)

31. *Crying in the Wilderness: Evangelism and Mission in Today's Culture*, Dr. David Smith (Paternoster, 2000), 52

32. *Living as the People*, 34

33. *The Theology of the Old Testament*, Vol 2, Walther Eichrodt (SCM 1967), 265

34. *Cinderella with Amnesia*, Michael Griffiths (IVP, 1975), 23

35. *Choruses from 'The Rock'*, Collected Poems, T.S. Eliot, 1909-62, (Faber, 1974)

36. *Cinderella with Amnesia*

37. *The Gospel in a Pluralist Society*, Lesslie Newbigin (SPCK, 1989), 222, 223

38. *Baptism in the Old Testament*, Paul Beaseley Murray (Macmillan 1963), 55-60

39. *God's Church*, A.M. Stibbs (IVP, 1959), 10

40. *Living as the People of God: The Relevance of Old Testament Ethics*, Christopher JH Wright (IVP, 1983)

41. ibid, 110

42. *The Social Pattern of Christian Groups in the First Century: some prolegomena to the study of New Testament ideas of social obligation*, Edwin Arthur Judge (Tyndale Press, 1960), 40

43. *Theology for the Community of God*, Stanley J. Grenz (1994), 591

44. *Cease Fire: Searching for Sanity in America's Culture Wars*, Tom Sine (Grand Rapids: Eerdmans 1995), 224

45. 'Can a Nation be Changed', Matt Redman, Copyright © 1996 Thankyou Music

46. Andrew Fuller, Carey's friend, quoted in *Crying in the Wilderness: Evangelism and Mission in Today's Culture*, David Smith (Paternoster, 2000), 2

47. *Crying in the Wilderness*

48. ibid, 13

49. ibid, 11

50. ibid, 21

51. *Facing the New Challenges*, John Mbiti (Kisumu, Kenya: Evangel Publishing, 1978)

52. *Transforming Society*, Melba Padilla Maggay (Regnum, 1994), 96

53. ibid, 100

54. *The Screwtape Letters*, Letter 2, C.S. Lewis (1942)

55. *Living as the People*

56. *Ten Commandments in Recent Research*, J.J. Stamm, M.E. Andrews (translator) (SCM Press, Feb 1967), 39

57. *Cinderella with Amnesia*, 7

58. *The Crown and the Fire*, Tom Wright

59. *A Search for God in Time and Memory: An Exploration Traced in the Lives of Individuals from Augustine to Sartre*, John S. Dunne (Macmillan, 1969), 7

60. *A History of Israel*, John Bright (SCM Press, 1981)

61. *The Grand Essentials*, Ben Patterson (World, 1987), 101

62. *Transforming Mission: Paradigm Shifts in Theology of Mission* (American Society of Missiology Series, No. 16), David Jacobus Bosch (Maryknoll, NY: Orbis, 1991), 353

63. *Story*, Brian D. McLaren, The Re-Evaluation Forum, Younger Leaders Network

64. *After Virtue: A Study in Moral Theory*, Alasdair MacIntyre, 2nd edn (London: Duckworth, 1994), 216

65. Jim Partridge is a local church leader and youth specialist, and until recently oversaw the youth ministry at Spring Harvest. His comments were offered as part of the theme development process for Spring Harvest 2007

66. *Emily of New Moon*, L.M. Montogomery (Laurel Leaf; Reissue edition, April 1, 1983)

67. *New Bible Commentary, Matthew*, R.T. France

68. Some suggest that the Pharisees were based only in Jerusalem but N.T. Wright disputes this (*The Challenge of Jesus*, N.T. Wright (SPCK), 37)

69. Philo, usually known as Philo the Jew (Philo Judaeus) or Philo of Alexandria (a city in Egypt with a large Jewish Diaspora population in Greco-Roman times), lived from about 20 BC to about AD 50. He is one of the most important Jewish authors of the Second Temple period of Judaism and was a contemporary of both Jesus and Paul.

70. *The Challenge*, 37

71. Mishnah Aboth 3:2

72. *This We Believe: The Good News of Jesus Christ for the World*, Ajith Fernando contrib. (Zondervan, 2000), 128

73. Quoted in *Crying in the Wilderness*, David Smith (Paternoster 2000), 62

74. ibid, 61

75. *Mr Holland's Opus*, 1995, directed by Stephen Herek

76. *The Wind in the Willows*, Kenneth Grahame (London: Methuen Children's Books Limited, Magnet Reprint, 1978), 155-156

77. This famous story is variously quoted, including in *The Trivialization of God*, 66, and *Searching for a God to Love*, Chris Blake (Word Press)

78. *Principles of Christian Theology*, John Macquarrie (SCM Press, 1966), 284

79. ibid, 276

80. *The Word of God and the Word of Man*, Karl Barth, Douglas Horton trans. (Hodder and Stoughton, 1928), 196

81. *The Epistle to the Romans*, Karl Barth, Edwin C. Hoskyns trans. (London: Oxford, 1933)

82. *Karl Barth: An Introduction to his Early Theology, 1910-1931*, Thomas F. Torrance (London: SCM, 1962), 31

83. Quoted in *The Lost Soul of American Politics*, John P. Diggins (New York: Basic, 1984), 7

84. Quoted in *Searching for a God to Love*, preface

85. *Old Testament Theology*, Vol. 1, Gerhard von Rad (Edinburgh and London: Oliver and Boyd, 1962), 205

86. *Teaching a Stone to Talk*, Annie Dillard (New York: Harper and Row, 1982), 40-41

87. *The Trivialization of God*, 13

88. *The Prophets*, Abraham Joshua Heschel (New York: Harper and Row, 1962), 227

89. *Open to Judgement: Sermons and Addresses*, Rowan Williams (Darton, Longman & Todd, 1994)

90. *Systematic Theology*, Augustus H. Strong (Philadelphia: Judson Press, 12th edition, 1949), 271

91. *The Problem of Pain*, C.S. Lewis (New York: Macmillan, 1962), 40-41

92. *Patterns of Discipleship in the New Testament*, Richard N. Longenecker ed. (Eerdmans, 1996)

93. Ernest Lucas, comments shared in theological feedback on an early draft of the Spring Harvest *Study Guide 2007*.

94. *Living as the People of God*

95. ibid, 27

96. *The Horse and His Boy*, C.S. Lewis (Middlesex: Puffin, 1954), 167-169

97. *The Trivialization of God*, 31

98. ibid, 37

99. U2, 'Yahweh', *How to Dismantle an Atomic Bomb*

100. 'Holiness in the Priestly Writings of the Old Testament', Philip Jensen, in *Holiness: Past and Present*, Stephen C. Barton ed. (T&T Clark), 99

101. *Spoken Worship*

102. *The Community of Shalom: God's Radical Alternative*, Jim Punton, adapted from an original paper presented at the FYT Conference in Leicester in 1975, Frontier Youth Trust, http://www.fyt.org.uk/pdf/shalom.pdf

103. Address by Brendan McAllister, Director of Mediation Northern Ireland, to the Scottish Mediation Conference in Glasgow on 4 March, 2005, http://www.mediationnorthernireland.org/documents/Scottish_Mediation_speeches_4_March_2005.pdf

104. Quoted in *Holiness: Past and Present*

105. *New Bible Dictionary*, Eds D.R.W. Wood, A.R. Millard, J.I. Packer, D.J. Wiseman, I. Howard Marshall (InterVarsity Press: Downers Grove, 1996, c1982, c1962)

106. *The Survivor: An Anatomy of Life in the Death Camps*, Terrence Des Pres (Oxford University Press, 1976), 53,57,66

107. *Faith after the Holocaust*, Eliezer Berkovits (New York: KTAV, 1973), 78-79

108. *Twenty Months at Auschwitz*, Pelagia Lewinska, quoted in *Different Voices: Women and the Holocaust*, Carol Ann Rittner and John K. Roth eds. (New York: Paragon Press, 1973), 87

109. *Holiness in Extremis: Jewish Women's Resistance to the Profane in Auschwitz*, Professor Melissa Raphael, in *Holiness: Past and Present*, 381

110. *I Have Lived a Thousand Years: Growing up in the Holocaust*, Livia Bitton-Jackson (London: Simon and Shuster, 1999), 83,92

111. *Holiness in Extremis*, 386

112. *The Return of the King: being the third part of The Lord of the Rings*, J.R.R. Tolkien (New York: Ballantine, 1965), 283

113. Quoted in *The King of the Hill*, Spring Harvest 2001 Study Guide, Jeff Lucas (Spring Harvest), 45

114. Quoted in *Searching for a God to Love*, 105

115. *The Way of Israel: Biblical Faith and Ethics*, James Muilenburg (Harper Torch Books, 1961)

116. *Deuteronomy*, Chris Wright (NIBC, Hendrickson/Paternoster 1996), 145

117. *Evangelism and Social Action*, Ronald J. Sider (Hodder and Stoughton, 1993), 141

118. *The Message of Mission*, Howard Peskett and Vinoth Ramachandra (IVP, 2003), 113

119. *Living as the People of God*, 147

120. *Good News to the Poor: The Gospel Through Social Involvement*, Tim Chester (IVP, 2004), 19

121. *The Message of Mission*, 112

122. *The Soul of Politics: A Practical and Prophetic Vision For Change*, Jim Wallis (Fount, 1994), 163

123. *Walking with the Poor*, 192

124. Seen on a personal visit to Addis Ababa by Jeff and Kay Lucas, 2006

125. *Walking with the Poor*, 192

126. ibid

127. For more on child focused development see *Child Focused Development: An Introduction*, Joachim Theis (SEAPRO Save the Children, May, 1996)

128. Quoted in 'Rwanda: Why?', John Martin, *Transformation* (12:2, 1995), 2 http://www.ocms.ac.uk/transformation/

129. 'Questions from Rwanda', Roger Bowen, *Transformation* (12:2, 1995), 17

130. Quoted in 'Rwanda: Why?'

131. *How Movies Helped Save My Soul: Finding Spiritual Fingerprints in Culturally Significant Films*, Gareth Higgins (Relevant Books, 2003)

132. Quoted in *Searching for a God to Love*, 117-118

133. 'Baptism, Eucharist, and Ministry – Faith and Order Paper No. 111', (Geneva: World Council of Churches, 1982), 20 http://www.oikoumene.org/index.php?id=2638 Quoted in *The People of God: An Orthodox Perspective*, George C. Papademetriou, http://www.goarch.org/en/ourfaith/articles/article9285.asp

134. *The Challenge of Jesus*

135. *Jerusalem in the Time of Jesus: An Investigation into Economic & Social Conditions During the New Testament Period*, Joachim Jeremias (Philadelphia: Fortress, 1975), 305, 311

136. *The Upside Down Kingdom*, 224

137. *God for Us: The Trinity and Christian Life*, Catherine Mowry LaCugna (San Francisco: HarperCollins, 1991), 401

138. *Rediscovering the Teaching of Jesus*, Norman Perrin (HarperCollins, 1969), 107

139. *Jesus the Jew*, Geza Vermes (Augsburg Fortress), 224

140. *Common Worship*, Holy Communion Eucharistic Prayer D (Archbishops' Council of the Church of England, 2000)

141. *Conflict, Holiness & Politics in the Teaching of Jesus,* Marcus J. Borg (Continuum International, 1998)

142. ibid, 100

143. *The Trial and Death of Jesus*, Haim Hermann Cohn (Ktav), 6

144. *Jesus and the Quest*, 100

145. *Saint Mark* (Pelican Gospel Commentary), D.E. Nineham (Penguin Books, 1969), 95

146. *From Politics to Piety: The Emergence of Pharisaic Judaism*, Jacob Nuesner (Wipf & Stock), 80

147. *Jesus and the Quest*, 96

148. ibid, 97

149. *The New Testament and Rabbinic Judaism*, David Daube (London, 1956), 170-75

150. *Jesus and the Quest*, 96

151. ibid, 96

152. *Law in the New Testament*, J. Duncan M. Derrett (Wipf & Stock), 208-227

153. *Parables of Jesus*, Eta Linnemann (SPCK), 111-112

154. *The Founder of Christianity*, C.H. Dodd (Fontana), 63-65

155. *Jerusalem in the Time of Jesus*, 375

156. *Rainbow Theology: Grace in Diversity*, 'The Blessing and the Challenge of a Global Church Family', Rose Dowsett, http://www.eauk.org/theology/key_papers/upload/EVANGEL%20-%20DOWSETT%20GLOBAL%20MISSION.pdf

157. *The Upside Down Kingdom*, 221

158. *Whose Reality Counts? Putting the First Last*, Robert Chambers (ITDG, 1997)

159. 'New Approaches to Children and Development', Michael Edwards (*Journal of International Development*, Introduction and Overview, 1996), 813-826

160. *Faith in a Changing Culture*, John Drane (Marshall Pickering, 1994), 124

161. Adapted from *Mission-shaped Children: Moving Towards a Child-centered Church*, Margaret Withers (Church House Publishing, 2006)

162. *Transforming Children into Spiritual Champions*, George Barna (USA, Regal Books, 2003), 66-7

163. ibid, 18, 34, 37

164. *Children in the Early Church*, W.A. Strange (Carlisle: Paternoster, 1996),113

165. *Children Finding Faith*, Francis Bridger (Milton Keynes: Scripture Union 2000), 8

166. *The Tide is Running Out*, Peter Brierley (London: Christian Research, 2000)

167. Quoted in *Perspectives on Children and the Gospel*, Ron Buckland (Australia: Scripture Union, 2001), 29

168. *Jesus and the Victory of God*, N.T. Wright (London: SPCK, 1996), 203

169. *The Provocative Church*, 40

170. For example see *Jesus and Jerusalem*, E.P. Sanders (London: SCM, 1985), 61-71

171. *The Great Reversal: Ethics and the New Testament*, Allen Verhey (Eerdmans, 1984), 13

172. *The Provocative Church*, 58

173. *The Eye of the Needle*, Roy McCloughry (Leicester: IVP, 1990), 123

174. *The Upside Down Kingdom*, 24

175. *The Provocative Church*, 51

176. *The Gospel in a Pluralist Society*, 132

177. *The Challenge of Jesus*, 27

178. *The Provocative Church*, 31

179. *Why Bother with Church?*, Simon Jones (IVP, 2001) 39

180. *Let my People Grow: Reflections on Making Disciples Who Make a Difference in Today's World*, Mark Greene and Tracy Cotterell eds (Authentic, 2006)

181. *Waterside*, Jeff Lucas

182. *Let my People Grow*

183. *Rainbow Theology*

184. ibid

185. *Mount Fuji and Mount Sinai: A Critique of Idols*, Kosuke Koyama (Orbis Books, 1985)

186. *Rainbow Theology*

187. ibid

188. Excerpted from 'The Black Church in the UK', Jonathan Oloyede, *Christianity Magazine* (October 2005)

189. *Café Theology*, Michael Lloyd (Alpha International 2005) 179

190. *Paul for Everyone*, N.T. Wright (SPCK, 2002) 27

191. *Christianity Magazine* (October 2005)

192. *Spoken Worship*

193. Quoted in *Being The Body*, Charles Colson and Ellen Vaughn (Word, 1992) 81

194. *Mission Theology Today*, John Power (Gill and Macmillan, 1970) 28

195. *Kirche und Volk in der deutschen Missionswissenschaft*, J.C. Hoekendijk (Munich: Christian Kaiser Verlag, 1967) 30-38

196. 'Neue Herrschaftverhaltnisse als Grund der Mission' in *Evangelical Theology* vol. 34, 462

197. *The Household of God*, Lesslie Newbigin (Paternoster, 1998) 81

198. *Faith in a Changing Culture*, 69

199. *Die formale Struktur von Mt. 28:18–20*, Gerhard Friedrich (1983)

200. *Transforming Mission*, 57

201. *The Bible and the Flag: Protestant Mission and British Imperialism in the 19th and 20th Centuries*, Brian Stanley (Leicester: Apollos, 1990)

202. *The Theology of the Sacraments*, Donald Macpherson Baillie (Faber and Faber, 1957) 69 .

203. Luke Bretherton, comments shared in theological feedback on 2007 Study Guide

204. *The Trivialization of God*, 30

205. 'Pastoral Ministry and the Place of the Sacraments', T.M. Moore, in *Reforming Pastoral Ministry*, John H Armstrong ed. (Wheaton: Crossway, 2001) 206

206. *The Gospel-Driven Church: Retrieving Classical Ministries for Contemporary Revivalism* (Deep Church Series), Ian Stackhouse (Paternoster, 2004) 133

207. *Words, Wonders and Power: Understanding Contemporary Christian Fundamentalism and Revivalism*, Martyn Percy (SPCK, 1996) 77-78

208. *Missions in State and Church*, Peter Taylor Forsyth (London: Hodder and Stoughton, 1908) 17

209. *A Guide to the Sacraments*, John Macquarrie (London: SCM, 1997) 139-140

210. *Worship in the Early Church*, Ralph P. Martin (Grand Rapids: Eerdmans, 1974) 126

211. *The Christian Faith: An Introduction to Christian Doctrine*, Colin E. Gunton (Oxford: Blackwell, 2002) 145

212. *The Lord's Supper in the New Testament*, A.J.B. Higgins (SCM, 1952) 54

213. *The Christian Faith*, Gunton

214. *Spoken Worship*, Kelly

215. *Christianity Magazine*, Jeff Lucas (December 2006)

216. *Walking with the Poor*, 206

217. 'How the World Lost its Story', Robert W. Jenson in *First Things*, vol. 36 (1993), 3 http://www.firstthings.com/ftissues/ft9310/articles/jenson.html

218. *The Provocative Church*, 66

219. *International Review of Missions* (LIV 1965), 455

220. *The Provocative Church*, 64

221. ibid, 67

222. *The Go-Between God: The Holy Spirit and the Christian Mission*, John V. Taylor (London: SCM, 1972), 3

223. *The Provocative Church*, 170

224. Quoted in *Walking with the Poor*, 210

225. *The Gospel in a Pluralist Society*, 132

226. *The Provocative Church*, 77-78

227. ibid, 63

228. *The Gospel in a Pluralist Society*, 132

229. *Christianity Rediscovered*, Vincent J. Donovan (Chicago: Fides, 1978), 22

230. *The Second Reformation: Reshaping the Church for the 21st Century*, William A. Beckham (Touch, 1995), 170

231. ibid, 170

232. *The Provocative Church*, 2

233. ibid, 2

234. ibid, 74

235. *Faith in a Changing Culture*, 109

236. *Understanding Religious Conversion*, Lewis R. Rambo (New Haven, CT: Yale, 1993), 165

237. *The Provocative Church*, 94

238. *Finding Faith Today*, John Finney (Bible Society, 1992), 25

239. Announcing the *Reign of God*, Mortimer Arias (Fortress, 1983), 3

240. *Evangelism: Doing Justice and Preaching Grace*, Harvie M. Conn (Grand Rapids: Zondervan, 1982), 32

241. *The Provocative Church*, 140

242. *Selected Poems*, R.S. Thomas (London: J.M. Dent, 1996) quoted also in *Crying in the Wilderness*, David Smith (Paternoster, 2000), 68

243. 'Early Church Catechesis and New Christians' Classes in Contemporary Evangelicalism', Clinton E. Arnold, *Journal of the Evangelical Theological Society* (March 2004) http://www.etsjets.org/jets/journal/47/47-1/47-1-pp039-054_JETS.pdf

244. *Didascalia Apostolorum*, R. Hugh Connolly (Oxford: Clarendon Press, 1929) http://www.bombaxo.com/didascalia.html cited in 'The Gospel and the Catechumenate in the Third Century', Paul F. Bradshaw, *Journal of Theological Studies 50* (1999), 143

245. *De Catechizandis Rudibus* (12.17)

246. 'Baptism, Catechism, and the Eclipse of Jesus' Teaching in Early Christianity', Alan Kreider, *Tyndale Bulletin* 47.2 (November 1996), 316–18

247. Michel Dujarer, *Catechumenate 64*, says 'it usually lasted three years.'

248. *The Apostolic Tradition of Hippolytus of Rome* was composed in approximately 215 in Rome http://www.bombaxo.com/hippolytus.html

249. *Early Christian Baptism and the Catechumenate*, Thomas M. Finn (Message of the Fathers of the Church 6; Collegeville, MN: Liturgical, 1992)

250. *Catechumenate 64*

251. *Augustine and the Catechumenate*, William Harmless (Pueblo Book; Collegeville, MN: Liturgical,1995)

252. Cited in *Augustine and the Catechumenate*

253. *The Apostolic Tradition* (39:1–2; see also 18:1–5; 19:1–2)

254. *Peregrinato 46*, Egeria, in 'Early Church Catechesis and New Christians' Classes in Contemporary Evangelicalism', Clinton E. Arnold

255. ibid. See 'Cyril of Jerusalem's Use of Scripture in Catechesis', Pamela Jackson, *Theological. Studies 52* (1991), 431–50

256. 'Catechesis,' Klaus Wegenast, *The Encyclopedia of Christianity* (Grand Rapids: Eerdmans, 1999), 1.360

257. *Preach the Word*, Greg Haslam ed., 'Preaching the Big Story,' chapter by Phillip Greenslade (Sovereign, 2006), 146

258. *The Household of God*, Leslie Newbigin (SCM Press, 1953), 25

One Holy, Catholic, Apostolic People